Table of Contents

Part 1: Foundations of Screenwriting

Part 2: Advanced Writing Techniques

Part 3: Screenwriting for Diverse Formats

Part 4: Mastering Visual and Auditory Elements

Chapter 14: Scene Construction and Visual Storytelling
- Learn how to construct scenes that drive narrative and captivate visually.
- Use AI to enhance previsualization and analyze visual storytelling flow.

Chapter 15: Dialogue That Resonates
- Craft dialogue that is authentic, engaging, and emotionally impactful.
- Use AI tools to refine tone, subtext, and rhythm.

Chapter 16: Sound and Music in Screenwriting
- Incorporate soundscapes and music cues into your scripts for emotional resonance.
- Learn how AI can suggest sound or musical motifs based on your story's tone.

Part 5: The Business of Screenwriting

Chapter 17: Breaking Into the Industry
- Navigate the screenwriting world, from Hollywood to indie markets.
- Use AI to build networking strategies and identify market trends.

Chapter 18: Pitching Your Script in the Digital Age
- Master techniques for crafting standout pitches and presentations.
- Use AI tools to tailor pitches for producers, studios, or streaming platforms.

Chapter 19: Legal and Ethical Considerations
- Understand copyright, ownership, and ethical practices in AI-assisted storytelling.

Chapter 20: Real-World AI Success Stories in Screenwriting
- Explore case studies of screenwriters leveraging AI to craft hit scripts.

Chapter 21: How to Self-Publish and Market Your Screenplay
- Learn strategies for independently publishing or marketing your screenplay.
- Use AI to create promotional materials and reach your target audience.

Part 6: AI-Assisted Creativity

Part 7: Case Studies and Future Trends

Appendices: Additional Resources for Screenwriters

- Character development sheets to deepen your understanding of motivations and arcs.
- Scene construction templates to streamline your writing process.
- Three-Act Structure and alternative framework mapping sheets.
- Logline and pitch crafting guides for quick and impactful presentations.

- Clear definitions of key screenwriting terminology, from "inciting incident" to "denouement."
- User-friendly explanations of AI terms, including "neural networks" and "audience simulation."

- AI tools for brainstorming, editing, and audience analysis.
- Industry-standard software for screenwriting and collaboration.
- Resources for finding agents, producers, and networking opportunities.

- Examples of AI-assisted dialogue enhancements.
- Comparisons of scene drafts before and after AI analysis.
- Visualizations of story pacing and emotional beats generated by AI tools.

- Reflect on the balance between AI-driven insights and human creativity.
- Reaffirm that AI is a tool to enhance, not replace, the writer's unique vision.
- Encourage readers to continue innovating and embracing new storytelling possibilities.

Introduction: Your Journey Begins Here

Every great film starts with a spark—an idea born from a fleeting moment of inspiration, a question that lingers, or a story that demands to be told. If you're holding this book, you already have that spark. You might even have a dream—one where your name appears in the opening credits of a screenplay that captivates the world. But between the spark and the screen lies a journey, one that can feel overwhelming without the right guidance. That's where this book comes in.

AI has read more scripts than any person could in a lifetime, studied the patterns of great storytelling, and uncovered the structures that resonate universally. But here's the truth: AI cannot replace the one thing that makes your story truly unique—your creativity. The imagination you bring to the page is irreplaceable. It's the soul of every great script, and no machine can replicate that. What AI can do, however, is amplify your talent, refine your ideas, and give you the tools to shape your vision into a screenplay that's ready to shine.

This book isn't just an instructional guide; it's a mentor. Think of it as your personal tutor, here to walk with you every step of the way. From crafting unforgettable characters to structuring scenes that take an audience's breath away, this book combines time-tested storytelling techniques with cutting-edge AI insights to help you turn your idea into a magical screenplay.

Inside these pages, you'll find answers to the questions that have kept you up at night. You'll learn how to bring out the best in your story, overcome writer's block, and craft a script that isn't just functional but transformative. You'll discover how to pitch your idea, navigate the industry, and even self-publish if that's your dream. Most importantly, you'll see that what feels impossible now is entirely within your reach.

This is more than a book—it's a journey of discovery. Together, we'll explore the boundless possibilities of your imagination and the structured frameworks that bring those possibilities to life. By the end of this journey, you won't just have a screenplay; you'll have the confidence, skills, and clarity to call yourself a screenwriter.
So turn the page, and let's begin turning your dream into reality.

Chapter 1: The Role of AI in Modern Screenwriting

In the past, the process of writing a screenplay was akin to traversing uncharted territory. Writers spent countless hours analyzing scripts, perfecting their craft through trial and error, and searching for that elusive key to success. Today, the world of screenwriting has changed. Artificial Intelligence (AI) is no longer just a futuristic concept—it's a creative partner, offering insights, tools, and guidance that were once unimaginable.

But what does that mean for you, the writer? Should you fear that AI might replace your creativity? Absolutely not. AI isn't here to take over; it's here to empower. It acts as a collaborator, capable of analyzing, suggesting, and streamlining the technical aspects of your work while leaving the imaginative and personal core—your unique creative voice—intact.

What AI Brings to the Table
1. Pattern Recognition from Thousands of Scripts
2. AI has read and analyzed more screenplays than any human ever could. It identifies patterns in successful scripts, such as story arcs, pacing, and audience engagement points. It recognizes what works, why it works, and how to replicate it— giving you a massive advantage.
3. Streamlining the Writing Process
4. From brainstorming to outlining and editing, AI tools can save time by helping with tedious tasks. For example:
   ○ Generate alternative storylines when you hit a roadblock.
   ○ Suggest improvements to pacing or dialogue authenticity.
   ○ Analyze character arcs for consistency and emotional resonance.
5. Real-Time Feedback
6. AI can provide instant feedback on your script, pointing out weak scenes, identifying dialogue that feels unnatural, or suggesting ways to tighten your structure. Think of it as having a trusted advisor available 24/7.
7. Unbiased Audience Simulation
8. But knowing what AI can do is just the beginning. To truly unlock its potential, you need to understand how to incorporate these tools into your writing process effectively. Whether you're brainstorming unique ideas, refining dialogue, or analyzing your story's pacing, AI is here to help at every step. Let's explore exactly how you can use AI to supercharge your screenwriting workflow.

How to Use AI Tools to Supercharge Your Writing Process
AI is more than a passive tool—it's an active collaborator that can enhance every stage of the screenwriting process. By integrating AI into your workflow, you can streamline brainstorming, refine your story structure, and polish your dialogue with precision. Here's how to apply AI-driven insights in practical ways:

1. Idea Generation
Struggling to find the right spark for your story? AI can help you explore new directions by generating variations on your initial idea or suggesting "what if" scenarios.
- Example Process: Input a basic concept into an AI brainstorming tool, such as:
  - "A heist movie with a supernatural twist."
  - AI Output:
    - "A team of ghosts robbing a bank."
    - "A thief who can rewind time during a heist."
    - "A cursed artifact forces its owner to commit crimes against their will."
- How to Apply: Use these suggestions to refine your premise or find a fresh angle.

2. Story Structure Analysis
AI tools can map your story's structure, highlighting where key beats like the inciting incident, midpoint, and climax occur. They can identify pacing gaps and suggest rearrangements to enhance narrative flow.
- Example Process: Upload an outline of your screenplay to an AI structure tool.
  - Feedback:
    - "The midpoint occurs too late, delaying the escalation of stakes."
    - "Act 1 introduces the protagonist effectively but lacks a clear inciting incident."
- How to Apply: Use the feedback to adjust scene placement or tighten your pacing.

3. Refining Dialogue

AI can analyze dialogue to ensure it feels authentic and aligns with each character's voice. It can also suggest alternative phrasings to add subtext or emotion.

- Example Process: Input a dialogue exchange:
  - Original:
    - John: "Why are you late again?"
    - Mary: "It's none of your business."
  - AI Suggestion:
    - John: "We can't keep doing this. Where were you?"
    - Mary: "Don't start, John. You don't want to know."
- How to Apply: Use AI-suggested dialogue as a starting point to add depth or tension.

4. Editing and Revisions

Editing is one of AI's strongest suits. AI can flag issues like redundant exposition, underdeveloped stakes, or inconsistencies in character arcs.

- Example Process: Upload your draft for analysis.
  - Feedback:
    - "The stakes in Act 2 are unclear. What happens if the protagonist fails?"
    - "The climax resolves too quickly. Consider extending the confrontation."
- How to Apply: Review the flagged sections and rewrite them with AI's insights in mind.

Practical Applications of AI in Screenwriting

While we've touched on how AI can assist in brainstorming, structure, dialogue, and editing, let's explore specific examples of how AI can enhance your writing process.

1. Brainstorming Unique Plot Twists

- Input: "A romantic comedy set in space."
- AI Suggestion:
  - "Two rival astronauts are stranded on a remote moon and must work together to survive—falling in love along the way."
- How It Helps: Sparks ideas that blend genres or explore unconventional scenarios.

2. Mapping Audience Engagement

- Use AI to simulate audience reactions at key moments in your script.
  - Example: "80% of simulated viewers lost engagement during a long exposition scene in Act 1."
  - Solution: Condense the exposition and show the same information visually.

3. Visualizing Story Pacing
AI tools can create a "tension map" of your screenplay, showing where stakes rise and fall.
- Example: The pacing dips for too long after the midpoint—add a subplot to maintain tension.
- How It Helps: Ensures your screenplay keeps audiences engaged.

Practical Exercise: AI in Action
To fully embrace the capabilities of AI, let's put it to work. Follow this simple exercise to experience how AI can inspire and refine your creative process:

Step 1: Create a One-Line Premise
Write a high-level concept for your screenplay.
- Example: "A detective who can hear the thoughts of animals solves a murder case."

Step 2: Use AI to Expand the Idea
Input your premise into an AI brainstorming tool and generate three alternative directions.
- AI Output:
  - "The detective discovers the animals are hiding their own secrets."
  - "The animals lead the detective to an underground conspiracy involving illegal experiments."
  - "The detective's ability begins to fade as they close in on the killer."

Step 3: Develop a Scene
Choose one idea and write a brief scene outline using AI's suggestions.
- Example Scene: The detective questions a nervous cat who saw the crime, but the cat demands a deal: protection from the neighborhood dog gang.

Step 4: Refine the Scene
Input the scene into an AI dialogue tool to polish the exchanges between the detective and the cat, ensuring the tone is consistent and engaging.

Partnering with AI to Enhance Creativity
AI isn't just a tool; it's a collaborator. By incorporating AI into your screenwriting process, you can uncover fresh ideas, streamline revisions, and maintain creative momentum. Remember, AI amplifies your unique vision—it doesn't replace it.

AI and the Creative Process
While AI excels at technical analysis, it cannot create the beating heart of your screenplay. The spark of an idea, the nuance of human emotion, and the depth of your characters all come from you. AI can only enhance these elements, never replace them.

Imagine a painter with a well-stocked studio. AI is like having all the brushes, colors, and techniques at your disposal. But it's your vision that brings the masterpiece to life. Whether you're writing a poignant drama or a laugh-out-loud comedy, your creativity is the guiding force, and AI is the tool to sharpen it.

Breaking Down Misconceptions
- AI is not "cheating."
- Using AI doesn't diminish your talent—it amplifies it. Just as a director uses advanced cameras or a musician uses sound-mixing software, a writer using AI is simply leveraging technology to enhance their craft.
- AI doesn't stifle originality.
- On the contrary, it can inspire it. By presenting you with alternative perspectives, unexpected plot twists, or novel ways to frame a scene, AI can push you to think in new and exciting ways.
- AI isn't a one-size-fits-all tool.
- Not every suggestion will fit your story, and that's okay. The power lies in your ability to decide what aligns with your vision and what doesn't.

Practical Applications of AI in Screenwriting
Let's look at a few examples of how AI can assist you throughout the screenwriting process:
- During Brainstorming: AI can generate prompts based on your initial idea, helping you explore "what if" scenarios you might not have considered.
- While Outlining: Tools can analyze your story structure to ensure it adheres to proven frameworks or suggest alternative paths for exploration.
- When Writing Dialogue: AI can analyze word choice, tone, and pacing, ensuring every line feels authentic to your characters.
- In Revision: AI highlights inconsistencies, redundancies, or pacing issues, streamlining the editing process.

What This Means for You

The rise of AI doesn't signal the end of traditional screenwriting—it marks the beginning of a new era. By embracing this technology, you'll gain tools to unlock your potential, refine your craft, and overcome challenges more efficiently than ever before.

The partnership between your creativity and AI's technical expertise can transform the way you write, offering opportunities to focus on the storytelling elements that matter most while automating the less glamorous aspects of the process.

Remember, the best stories don't come from machines. They come from the human spirit—the dreams, struggles, and ideas that only you can bring to the page. This book is your guide to merging the timeless art of storytelling with the boundless possibilities of AI, helping you turn your screenplay into something truly magical.

Chapter 2: Screenwriting Fundamentals

Before AI can help refine your ideas, and before your creativity can bring a story to life, it's essential to master the basics. Screenwriting is both an art and a craft, and like any craft, it has its rules and structures. Understanding these fundamentals is the foundation upon which great scripts are built. This chapter will guide you through the essential elements of a screenplay, offering clarity and confidence as you start your journey.

What Is a Screenplay?
A screenplay, often called a script, is more than just a collection of words—it's a blueprint for a film. It bridges your vision as a writer with the collaborative efforts of directors, actors, cinematographers, and editors. While a novel might describe every detail in flowing prose, a screenplay is concise, designed to communicate action and dialogue efficiently.

Think of it as an architectural plan. It sketches out the structure and flow but leaves room for interpretation by the collaborators who will bring it to life.

Core Elements of a Screenplay
To write a screenplay, you need to master its building blocks. These elements form the language of filmmaking:

1. Scene Headings (Sluglines)
   - Define where and when the action happens.
   - Example: INT. COFFEE SHOP – DAY (Interior, Coffee Shop, Day).
   - Keep it concise and visually oriented, giving the reader an immediate sense of location and time.

2. Action Lines
   - Describe what happens on screen. Action lines should be short, vivid, and cinematic.
   - Example: A steaming cup of coffee lands on the counter. The barista glances nervously at the clock.
   - Understanding the elements of a screenplay is essential, but crafting effective scenes requires more than just following the rules. Each scene must have a clear purpose, contribute to the story's progression, and engage the audience. Let's explore how to ensure your scenes are both purposeful and impactful.

3. Dialogue
- This is what your characters say. Keep it authentic, concise, and relevant to the story.
- Example:
- JANE
- (laughing)
- "You really think this is going to work?"

4. Parentheticals
- Brief instructions under the character's name to clarify their tone or action.
- Example: (whispering) or (angrily). Use sparingly to let dialogue and action shine.

5. Transitions
- Indicate how one scene moves to the next. While modern scripts use transitions sparingly, they're still useful for clarity in pivotal moments.
- Example: CUT TO: or FADE OUT.

Building Effective Scenes with AI Insights
A screenplay is more than a collection of scenes—it's a sequence of moments, each driving the story forward. To craft scenes that captivate and contribute to the overall narrative, consider these key elements:

1. The Purpose of a Scene
Every scene must serve one or more of the following purposes:
- Advance the Plot: Reveal new information, introduce conflicts, or resolve story threads.
- Example: In The Godfather, the restaurant assassination scene propels Michael Corleone further into the world of organized crime.
- Develop Characters: Show how characters grow, change, or reveal hidden aspects of their personalities.
- Example: In The Dark Knight, Bruce Wayne's conversation with Alfred about the Joker reveals his deep internal conflict.
- Establish Tone or Theme: Reinforce the story's emotional or philosophical underpinnings.
- Example: The opening montage in Up sets the tone for a story about love, loss, and resilience.

AI Application: Upload your scene outline to an AI tool that analyzes whether each scene fulfills at least one purpose. AI feedback might suggest combining or cutting scenes that lack impact.

2. Creating Scene Goals and Stakes

Scenes become compelling when characters have clear goals and encounter obstacles that create stakes.

How to Define Scene Goals:
- What does the character want?
- What's stopping them from getting it?
- What are the consequences of failure?

Example:

In Jurassic Park, the T. rex escape scene has clear stakes: survival. The characters' goal is to avoid the predator, and the obstacle is the chaos of the malfunctioning park.

AI Application: AI can highlight scenes where stakes feel flat or repetitive, suggesting ways to heighten tension.

3. Pacing Within and Between Scenes

Pacing ensures that scenes flow smoothly and maintain the audience's engagement.
- Scene-Level Pacing: Balancing moments of action with quieter, reflective beats.
- Example: In Mad Max: Fury Road, high-octane chases are punctuated by brief moments of stillness to let the audience catch their breath.
- Script-Wide Pacing: Distributing tension peaks and valleys throughout the screenplay.
- Example: In The Hunger Games, the slow build to the arena contrasts sharply with the fast-paced action of the Games.

AI Application: AI tools can map out the rhythm of your screenplay, identifying slow patches or overly long action sequences. They might suggest adding reflective scenes or tightening dialogue-heavy sections.

4. Transitions and Scene Flow

Seamless transitions between scenes keep the story cohesive.
- Use visual callbacks or emotional continuity to connect scenes.
- Example: The match cut in Lawrence of Arabia (blowing out a match to reveal the sunrise over the desert) bridges two locations while maintaining thematic coherence.

AI Application: AI can analyze transitions and suggest where abrupt shifts might confuse or disengage the audience. For example, if a tonal shift feels jarring, AI might recommend adjusting the scene order.

Practical Exercise: Crafting Purposeful Scenes
- Choose a scene from your screenplay or outline. Write down:
  - The scene's goal.
  - The stakes involved.
  - The transition leading to or from this scene.
- Input the scene into an AI tool for analysis. Note its feedback on pacing, stakes, and transitions.
- Revise the scene based on this feedback, ensuring it drives the story forward.

Formatting Basics
Industry professionals expect screenplays to follow a standard format. Proper formatting shows you're serious about your craft and makes your work easier to read and evaluate.

- Font: Use Courier or Courier New, 12-point size. This font ensures one page of your script roughly equals one minute of screen time.
- Margins: Use standard screenplay margins: 1.5 inches on the left and 1 inch on the right, top, and bottom.
- Page Length: Aim for 90–120 pages for feature films. Shorter scripts are better suited for TV pilots or indie projects.
- Page Numbers: Start numbering pages from Page 2, placing the number at the top right corner.

The Purpose of Every Scene
Every scene in your screenplay should serve a purpose. It must either:

- Advance the Plot: Move the story forward by revealing information, resolving conflicts, or introducing new challenges.
- Develop Characters: Show their growth, struggles, or relationships.
- Establish Tone or Theme: Deepen the audience's connection to the story world.

A scene that doesn't do at least one of these is likely unnecessary.

Balancing Show vs. Tell

One of the cardinal rules of screenwriting is "show, don't tell." Instead of explaining everything to the audience, let your visuals and dialogue reveal what's happening.

Example – Telling:
John feels angry about being ignored.

Example – Showing:
John slams the door, his face flushes red. He glares at the others, who continue their conversation as if he isn't there.

Showing allows the audience to infer emotions and motives, making the story more immersive and dynamic.

The Golden Rule: Keep It Visual

Film is a visual medium. Your job as a screenwriter is to write what can be seen or heard—not internal thoughts or abstract concepts. For instance:

- Instead of: "Sarah feels hopeful."
- Write: "Sarah glances at the sunrise, a small smile breaking across her face."

The First Page: Making an Impression

Your first page is your first impression. In today's competitive landscape, it's crucial to grab your reader's attention immediately.

- Start with a compelling visual or action.
- Introduce a character with a memorable moment.
- Hint at the story's tone or stakes early on.

Example – The Dark Knight
The opening scene with the bank heist immediately establishes the stakes, tone, and chaos of the story, pulling the audience in before they've met the protagonist.

Common Mistakes to Avoid

- Overloading Action Lines: Avoid describing every detail—let the director and actors interpret some elements.
- Dialogue Overload: Conversations should flow naturally, not feel like an information dump.
- Ignoring Formatting Standards: Sloppy formatting distracts from your story.

How AI Enhances the Fundamentals
Even with a solid understanding of the basics, mistakes happen, and that's where AI can help:

- Scene Analysis: AI tools can flag overwritten scenes, excessive dialogue, or inconsistent pacing.
- Formatting Assistance: AI ensures your script adheres to industry standards.
- Dialogue Polishing: AI identifies clunky dialogue and suggests alternatives that fit your character's voice.

Conclusion: Building Your Foundation
Mastering the fundamentals is the first step in your screenwriting journey. Every great script—whether a sweeping epic or an intimate indie—rests on a solid foundation of craft. AI can act as your safety net, ensuring you adhere to the basics while you focus on the heart of your story.

Now that you've built your foundation, it's time to move beyond the basics and dive into story structures that will bring your vision to life. Let's explore that in the next chapter.

Chapter 3: The Three-Act Structure and Beyond

Every story, no matter how innovative or experimental, has a structure that guides it from beginning to end. Structure provides a framework, a set of boundaries within which creativity can thrive. While the Three-Act Structure has long been the cornerstone of storytelling, modern narratives often combine or subvert traditional frameworks to keep audiences engaged.

In this chapter, we'll explore the fundamentals of the Three-Act Structure, delve into alternative storytelling methods, and discover how AI can assist in crafting, refining, and analyzing your story's structure.

Why Structure Matters

Imagine building a house without a blueprint. Without structure, even the most imaginative idea can collapse under its own weight. A well-structured screenplay:
1. Engages the Audience: Keeps them emotionally invested.
2. Ensures Pacing: Balances action, tension, and resolution.
3. Clarifies Intent: Helps collaborators (directors, actors, producers) understand your vision.

The Three-Act Structure

The Three-Act Structure divides your story into three key sections:

Act 1: Setup (25%)

This is where the foundation of your story is laid.
- Purpose: Introduce the protagonist, their world, and the central conflict.
- Key Moment: The Inciting Incident disrupts the status quo, setting the story in motion.
- Questions to Ask:
  o What does the protagonist want?
  o What's stopping them from getting it?

Example:
In The Matrix, Neo's monotonous life is shattered when he encounters Morpheus and learns the truth about the Matrix. The Inciting Incident—choosing the red pill—propels him into an entirely new world.

Act 2: Confrontation (50%)

The bulk of your story takes place here, where the stakes rise and the conflict deepens.
- Purpose: Develop relationships, introduce subplots, and show the protagonist struggling to achieve their goal.
- Key Moment: The Midpoint, a significant turning point that shifts the protagonist's focus or raises the stakes.
- Questions to Ask:
  - How is the protagonist changing or growing?
  - What obstacles increase the tension?

Example:
In Jurassic Park, the wonder of the park gives way to terror as the dinosaurs escape. The Midpoint (the T. rex's breakout) escalates the stakes and sets up the survivors' fight for survival.

Act 3: Resolution (25%)

The climax brings the story to its highest tension, followed by a resolution that ties up loose ends.
- Purpose: Deliver the payoff and show the protagonist overcoming or succumbing to their challenges.
- Key Moment: The Climax, where the story reaches its emotional and narrative peak.
- Questions to Ask:
  - Has the protagonist achieved their goal?
  - How has the world or protagonist changed?

Example:
In Die Hard, John McClane faces off against Hans Gruber in a final showdown, saving his wife and restoring order.

Beyond the Three-Act Structure
While the Three-Act Structure offers a proven framework, the emotional and thematic resonance of your screenplay depends on how well the theme aligns with key story beats and whether the stakes escalate effectively. Let's explore how to integrate these elements into your script and ensure your story remains engaging throughout.

Integrating Theme, Stakes, and Audience Engagement
While story structure serves as the skeleton of your screenplay, the theme and stakes provide its emotional core. A compelling screenplay aligns these elements seamlessly, ensuring every beat resonates with the audience.

1. Aligning Theme with Structure
Your screenplay's theme is its central idea—the message or question it explores. A well-executed theme ties together character arcs, major plot points, and even dialogue.

Steps to Align Theme:
1. Identify your theme.
   o Example: Redemption (The Shawshank Redemption), sacrifice (Avengers: Endgame), or love (Titanic).
2. Map key story beats to the theme.
   o Inciting Incident: Introduce the theme through the protagonist's dilemma.
   o Midpoint: Reinforce the theme with a turning point or revelation.
   o Climax: Resolve the theme through the protagonist's final decision or transformation.

Example:
In The Shawshank Redemption, the theme of hope is introduced when Andy refuses to give in to despair, reinforced by his actions throughout the story, and culminates in his triumphant escape and letter to Red.

AI Application: Use AI to analyze your story's consistency with its theme. For example, AI might flag moments where a scene feels disconnected from the overarching message.

2. Raising and Escalating Stakes
Stakes are the consequences of success or failure for your protagonist. Effective stakes are:
- Personal: Affecting the protagonist directly.
- Example: In A Quiet Place, survival stakes impact the family's daily life.
- Interpersonal: Affecting relationships between characters.
- Example: In Frozen, Elsa's powers put her sister Anna in danger.
- Global: Affecting the world or setting.
- Example: In Avengers: Infinity War, the stakes are the survival of half the universe.

Escalating Stakes:
- Stakes should increase as the story progresses.
- Start small (personal goals), then expand to larger consequences.
- Example: In The Hunger Games, Katniss's initial goal is survival, but by the climax, she's risking her life to save others and defy the Capitol.

AI Application: AI can map the stakes in your screenplay and highlight flat sections where tension diminishes. It might suggest ways to intensify conflicts or consequences.

3. Engaging the Audience Through Pacing and Emotional Beats
Audience engagement depends on balancing tension and release, ensuring your screenplay takes viewers on an emotional journey.

Pacing Techniques:
- Alternate high-stakes scenes with quieter moments to maintain engagement.
- Example: In Inception, high-action dream heists are interspersed with reflective scenes about Cobb's past.
- Build tension gradually, leading to major climaxes.
- Example: The Dark Knight slowly escalates the Joker's plans until chaos engulfs Gotham.

Emotional Beats:
- Identify moments where the audience should feel specific emotions (e.g., fear, hope, sadness).
  - Example: In Inside Out, the emotional beats align with Riley's struggles, creating a deeply resonant story.

AI Application: AI tools can simulate audience reactions, showing where emotional engagement dips and suggesting adjustments.

Practical Exercise: Mapping Theme and Stakes
- Define Your Theme: Write a one-sentence description of your screenplay's central idea.
  - Example: "Hope can flourish even in the darkest circumstances."
- Identify Thematic Beats: Map how each act reflects the theme.
  - Act 1: Introduce the theme through the protagonist's flaw.
  - Act 2: Explore the theme through conflict or a mentor's guidance.
  - Act 3: Resolve the theme through the protagonist's transformation.

- Evaluate Stakes: Write down the stakes in your screenplay at the beginning, midpoint, and climax.
  - Use AI to analyze whether stakes escalate consistently.
- Revise and Test: Adjust scenes where stakes feel flat or disconnected from the theme.

The Hero's Journey
Joseph Campbell's Hero's Journey expands on the Three-Act Structure by emphasizing the protagonist's transformation through 12 stages. Each stage represents a key moment in the hero's arc, showcasing their growth and challenges along the way.

1. The Ordinary World
The hero begins in their everyday life, where they are unaware of the adventure to come.
- Example: Harry Potter lives under the stairs at the Dursleys'.

2. The Call to Adventure
The hero is drawn into a new world or faces a challenge they cannot ignore.
- Example: Harry receives his Hogwarts letter, inviting him to a magical world.

3. Refusal of the Call
The hero initially hesitates, reluctant to leave their comfort zone or face the unknown.
- Example: Frodo hesitates to take the Ring to Mordor.

4. Meeting the Mentor
The hero encounters a mentor who provides guidance, tools, or encouragement for the journey ahead.
- Example: Obi-Wan Kenobi gives Luke Skywalker his father's lightsaber and introduces him to the Force.

5. Crossing the Threshold
The hero commits to the journey, leaving their familiar world behind.
- Example: Neo chooses the red pill and enters the Matrix.

6. Tests, Allies, and Enemies
The hero faces challenges, makes friends, and confronts foes, learning about the new world.
- Example: Katniss Everdeen builds alliances and faces threats in the Hunger Games arena.

7. Approach to the Inmost Cave
The hero prepares for the major challenge, often facing their deepest fears.
- Example: Simba returns to Pride Rock to confront Scar.

8. The Ordeal
The hero faces their greatest challenge, risking everything to achieve their goal.
- Example: Frodo resists the Ring's power while standing at the edge of Mount Doom.

9. The Reward (Seizing the Sword)
Having overcome the ordeal, the hero gains a reward—an object, insight, or new strength.
- Example: Harry retrieves the Philosopher's Stone and prevents Voldemort's return.

10. The Road Back
The hero must return to the ordinary world, often facing challenges along the way.
- Example: Dorothy returns to Kansas after defeating the Wicked Witch of the West.

11. The Resurrection
The hero faces one final test, where they demonstrate the growth and transformation from their journey.
- Example: Simba confronts Scar in the final battle, reclaiming his place as king.

12. Return with the Elixir
The hero brings newfound wisdom, strength, or resources back to their ordinary world to share with others.
- Example: Katniss returns home to District 12 as a symbol of rebellion and hope.

Why It Matters in Screenwriting
The Hero's Journey is a timeless narrative structure that resonates deeply with audiences because it mirrors universal experiences of growth, struggle, and transformation. Understanding and integrating these 12 stages into your screenplay can help create a compelling and emotionally impactful story.

The Puzzle Box Structure
Used in films like Inception and Westworld, this structure weaves multiple timelines or mysteries that gradually unfold.
AI's Role:
- Identify how plot threads interact.
- Flag potential confusion in overlapping timelines.

The Five-Act Structure
This format, popular in TV dramas and Shakespearean plays, divides the story into:
- Exposition
- Rising Action
- Climax
- Falling Action
- Denouement

Example:
Breaking Bad episodes often use this structure to create multiple peaks of tension.

Hybrid and Nonlinear Approaches
Some stories defy traditional rules, using fragmented timelines or experimental formats.

Example: Memento tells its story backward, mirroring the protagonist's fractured memory.

How AI Enhances Story Structure
AI can play a critical role in perfecting your screenplay's structure:
- Pacing Analysis: Identifies slow or rushed sections.
- Gap Detection: Highlights missing beats in frameworks like the Hero's Journey.
- Audience Simulation: Predicts emotional responses to key moments.
- Scene Rearrangement Suggestions: Ensures clarity in nonlinear storytelling.

Choosing the Right Structure for Your Story
Not all stories are suited to the same framework. Consider:
- Genre: Action films thrive on the Three-Act Structure, while dramas may favor the Five-Act Structure.
- Audience: Younger audiences may prefer fast-paced, straightforward structures; cinephiles may enjoy layered, puzzle-like narratives.
- Themes: Choose a structure that complements your story's emotional core.

Common Pitfalls in Structuring a Screenplay
- Underdeveloped Act 2: Avoid turning the middle of your screenplay into filler. Use subplots and character development to maintain momentum.
- Weak Inciting Incident: Ensure your Act 1 effectively hooks the audience.
- Rushed Resolution: Give your Act 3 the space it needs to deliver a satisfying payoff.

Practical Exercises to Apply Story Structures
- Break Down a Favorite Film
  - Identify its Acts, Inciting Incident, Midpoint, and Climax.
  - Consider how the structure contributes to the story's effectiveness.
- Experiment with Alternatives
  - Rewrite a short scene using a nonlinear approach or Puzzle Box framework.
- Map Your Story to Multiple Frameworks
  - Use the Three-Act Structure and Hero's Journey to outline your idea. Reflect on which fits better.

Conclusion: Structure as a Creative Tool
Story structure is not a cage—it's a guide. Mastering frameworks like the Three-Act Structure and experimenting with alternatives allows you to tailor your screenplay to its unique needs. AI enhances this process, offering insights and optimizations that ensure your story resonates with its audience.

Now that we've explored how to structure your screenplay, it's time to focus on the spark that will set it apart: a high-concept idea. In the next chapter, we'll dive into developing pitchable stories that captivate producers and audiences alike, turning your unique concept into a marketable masterpiece.

Chapter 4: High-Concept Ideas and Pitchable Stories

Some screenplays captivate attention not just through execution but because of the brilliance of their core idea. These are high-concept stories—the kind that spark excitement with just a sentence or two. They make agents, producers, and audiences immediately curious and eager to know more.

In this chapter, we'll explore what makes a screenplay high-concept, how to craft and refine such ideas, and how AI can assist in generating, testing, and tailoring these concepts for market success.

What Is a High-Concept Idea?
A high-concept idea is one that can be summed up in a single sentence and has immediate, widespread appeal. It's clear, compelling, and universally intriguing. High-concept ideas thrive on their ability to spark curiosity, deliver unique premises, and promise an engaging experience.

Characteristics of High-Concept Ideas:
1. A Unique Premise: Fresh, innovative, and attention-grabbing.
2. Broad Appeal: A concept that resonates across genres and demographics.
3. Clear Stakes: A central conflict or question that captivates the audience.

Examples of High-Concept Ideas:
- Jurassic Park: What if scientists cloned dinosaurs and opened a theme park?
- Inception: What if a thief could infiltrate dreams to plant ideas?
- A Quiet Place: What if deadly creatures hunted anyone who made a sound?

Why High-Concept Ideas Work
High-concept stories stand out because they combine creativity with clarity, making them:
1. Instantly Marketable: Easy to pitch and understand.
2. Curiosity-Inducing: They leave the audience eager to know how the story unfolds.
3. Scalable Across Formats: Often adaptable into franchises, sequels, or even different media.

Crafting High-Concept Ideas
Great high-concept ideas don't just appear—they're crafted by combining creativity with thoughtful exploration. Here's how to create your own:

1. Start with "What If" Questions
"What if" questions are the foundation of many high-concept ideas:
- What if humanity discovered a way to bring dinosaurs back to life? (Jurassic Park)
- What if someone woke up every day to repeat the same 24 hours? (Groundhog Day)

2. Combine Contrasting Elements
Fresh ideas often come from unexpected combinations:
- What if zombies were romantic? (Warm Bodies)
- What if superheroes lived in a realistic, gritty world? (The Dark Knight)

3. Elevate the Ordinary
Take a common scenario and add extraordinary stakes:
- What if a family was forced to live in complete silence to survive? (A Quiet Place).

Adapting High-Concept Ideas for Different Mediums
Not every high-concept idea fits neatly into a feature film format. Consider whether your story might thrive as:
- A Series: Longer formats like TV or streaming allow for deeper character arcs and complex storylines.
- A Short Film: Ideal for experimental or contained ideas.
- Interactive Media: Perfect for branching narratives or audience-driven decisions, like Bandersnatch.

Using AI to Develop High-Concept Ideas
AI is a powerful brainstorming tool that can help generate, refine, and tailor high-concept ideas.

1. Idea Generation
Input a basic idea or theme into AI, and it can provide variations or unexpected twists:
- Example: Input "time travel," and AI might suggest, What if time travel was only possible through dreams?

2. Trend Analysis
AI can analyze industry data to identify current trends:
- What genres or themes are popular?
- Which audience demographics are driving market demand?

3. Testing Ideas
AI can simulate audience reactions to your pitch or logline, helping you refine its appeal.

4. Avoiding Oversaturation
AI tools can check whether your concept feels too similar to existing films and suggest ways to make it unique.

Creating Pitchable Stories
A great idea needs to be presented effectively to capture attention. Here's how to craft a pitchable story:

1. The One-Sentence Pitch
Condense your idea into a single, compelling sentence:
- Formula:
- [Protagonist] must [goal] before [stakes].
  - Example: A paleontologist must survive when cloned dinosaurs escape at a theme park. (Jurassic Park)

2. The Logline
Expand slightly to provide context while maintaining clarity:
- Formula:
- When [inciting incident], a [protagonist] must [goal], or else [stakes].
  - Example: When a young boy discovers he's a wizard, he must attend a magical school and defeat an evil sorcerer who killed his parents. (Harry Potter)

3. Adding a Visual or Auditory Hook
High-concept pitches often succeed by evoking striking imagery or sound:
- "Dinosaurs roar back to life in a theme park." (Jurassic Park)
- "A blaring foghorn warns the family in silence of the unseen monsters outside." (A Quiet Place)

AI for Tailored Pitches
AI can adapt pitches to different audiences or platforms:
- Studio Executives: Focus on franchise potential and commercial viability.
- Indie Producers: Highlight emotional depth and artistic merit.
- Streaming Platforms: Emphasize bingeability or episodic potential.

Common Pitfalls and How to Avoid Them
- Overcomplicating the Premise:
- High-concept ideas thrive on simplicity. If it takes too long to explain, refine it.
- Lack of Emotional Depth:
- Even the most intriguing premise needs relatable characters and stakes.
- Too Similar to Existing Stories:
- AI tools can help ensure originality by flagging overused tropes.

Exercises to Refine Your High-Concept Ideas
- Write 10 "What If" Questions:
- Choose one and expand it into a one-sentence pitch.
- Combine Genres:
- Take two genres (e.g., romantic comedy + horror) and brainstorm ideas that blend their elements.
- Pitch Testing:
- Use AI to refine your pitch and logline. Test it on friends or fellow writers for feedback.

Checklist for Pitchable Screenplays
Before finalizing your idea, ask:
- Is the premise unique and engaging?
- Does it have broad appeal or a clear target audience?
- Can it be summarized in one or two sentences?
- Does it include a strong visual or emotional hook?

Conclusion: High-Concept Stories as Your Gateway
A high-concept idea is your screenplay's ticket to success. By combining creativity with clarity, crafting a strong pitch, and leveraging AI tools, you can create stories that capture the imagination of producers and audiences alike.

In the next chapter, we'll shift focus to the heart of any screenplay: the characters. Learn how to create compelling individuals who bring your high-concept idea to life.

Chapter 5: Writing Compelling Characters

At the heart of every great screenplay are its characters. They are the lenses through which the audience experiences the story, the anchors that evoke emotional connection, and the engines that drive the narrative forward. But crafting compelling characters requires more than just giving them names and roles—it demands depth, complexity, and relatability.

In this chapter, we'll dive deep into the art of creating memorable characters, explore their psychological makeup, and show how AI tools can refine and elevate your writing.

1. Understanding the Core of a Great Character
Compelling characters feel real. They aren't perfect—they are flawed, dynamic, and layered. At their core, great characters have:
- Relatability: Audiences connect to their struggles, fears, and dreams.
- Depth: They have backstories, desires, and conflicts, both internal and external.
- Dynamic Growth: They change throughout the story, often in unexpected but believable ways.

Example:
Tony Stark in Iron Man begins as a self-centered billionaire but evolves into a self-sacrificing hero. His vulnerability and wit make him relatable, while his transformation drives the narrative.

2. Archetypes and Breaking the Mold
Archetypes are timeless character templates that provide a foundation for storytelling. However, compelling characters often transcend these templates.

Common Archetypes
- The Hero: Overcomes challenges and grows into a better version of themselves. (Luke Skywalker in Star Wars)
- The Mentor: Guides the hero with wisdom and experience. (Yoda in Star Wars)
- The Shadow: Represents the darker aspects of the hero's personality or the story's antagonist. (Darth Vader in Star Wars)

Breaking the Mold
Subverting archetypes creates fresh, complex characters:
- The Reluctant Mentor: A mentor who resents their role (Haymitch in The Hunger Games).
- The Sympathetic Antagonist: An antagonist whose goals are understandable (Killmonger in Black Panther).

3. Building Depth: Goals, Motivations, and Flaws
Every character's actions should stem from their goal (what they want), motivation (why they want it), and flaws (what holds them back).

Goals vs. Needs
Characters often pursue external goals while grappling with internal needs.
- Example: In Finding Nemo, Marlin's goal is to find his son, but his need is to overcome his fear of loss and control.

Flaws as Relatability
Flaws make characters human. Audiences connect with imperfection:
- Sherlock Holmes: His brilliance is offset by arrogance and emotional detachment.
- Elsa in Frozen: Her fear of her powers isolates her.

AI Tool: AI can suggest personality traits and conflicts to create multidimensional characters.

Character Psychology and Inner Conflict
Great characters don't just face external challenges—they wrestle with inner conflicts that mirror their journeys. Exploring these psychological dimensions can create richer, more relatable individuals.

A. Needs vs. Wants
Characters often pursue external wants while grappling with internal needs.
- Wants: What the character thinks they want.
- Example: In Moana, Moana wants to prove herself by venturing beyond the reef.
- Needs: What the character truly needs to grow.
- Example: Moana needs to embrace her identity as the chosen one who will restore the heart of Te Fiti.

AI Application: AI can analyze your character arcs to ensure their wants and needs are in tension, driving emotional resonance.

B.. Internal Conflict
Internal conflict is the struggle between competing desires, fears, or values within a character.
- Example: In Breaking Bad, Walter White is torn between his desire to protect his family and his growing pride in his criminal empire.

Practical Exercise:
- Identify a key internal conflict for your protagonist. Write a scene where this conflict influences their decision-making.
- Use AI to simulate alternative outcomes, exploring how the decision impacts their arc.

Exploring Diversity and Representation
Modern audiences expect authentic and diverse characters that reflect the complexity of the real world. Writing characters from different cultural, social, or personal backgrounds requires research and nuance.

1. Moving Beyond Stereotypes
Avoid reducing characters to clichés or relying on tokenism.
- Example: Instead of portraying an LGBTQ+ character solely as comedic relief, give them a multidimensional personality and role in the plot.

2. Writing Across Cultures
If writing outside your lived experience, invest in thorough research and seek feedback from people within that culture.
- Example: In Black Panther, the representation of Wakandan culture draws on real African traditions while creating a futuristic, fictional society.

AI Application: AI tools can analyze characters for potential biases or suggest ways to deepen representation.

3. Creating Inclusive Narratives
Diversity isn't just about individual characters—it's about the interplay of perspectives across your screenplay.
- Example: In Everything Everywhere All at Once, the diverse cast and narrative explore universal themes through specific cultural lenses.

Practical Exercise:
- Write a character profile for someone outside your personal experience. Use AI to simulate dialogue or provide cultural context to ensure authenticity.

Nontraditional Characters
Compelling characters don't have to be human—or even alive.
Many screenplays feature nontraditional characters that evoke
emotion and drive the story.

1. Non-Human Characters
Characters like WALL-E or Gollum show how non-humans can be
relatable by giving them human-like desires, flaws, and growth.
- Example: In WALL-E, the titular robot's longing for
  connection mirrors universal human experiences.

2. Abstract Concepts as Characters
Abstract entities, such as Death in The Book Thief, can embody
themes and add depth to the story.
- Example: In Inside Out, Joy and Sadness are personifications
  of emotions, exploring how they coexist in human experience.

AI Application: Use AI to develop unique traits and arcs for
nontraditional characters, ensuring they resonate emotionally with
the audience.

Practical Exercise: Layering Your Characters
- Write a scene where your protagonist faces a decision
  influenced by both their internal conflict and external stakes.
- Identify how their actions reflect their goals, motivations, and
  flaws.
- Use AI to simulate alternative outcomes for the decision and
  analyze how these choices affect the character's arc.

4. Transformative Moments in Character Arcs
A compelling character arc involves meaningful change over the
course of the story.

Types of Character Arcs
- Positive Arc: The character grows or improves. (Frodo in The
  Lord of the Rings)
- Negative Arc: The character descends into darkness. (Walter
  White in Breaking Bad)
- Flat Arc: The character remains consistent but impacts the
  world around them. (Indiana Jones)

The Role of Key Decisions
Transformative moments often hinge on decisions that reflect
growth or regression.
- Example: In The Dark Knight, Bruce Wayne chooses to
  protect Gotham even at great personal cost.

5. Writing Unique and Authentic Dialogue
Dialogue is a powerful tool to reveal character personality, relationships, and emotional states.

Techniques for Effective Dialogue
- Match Speech to Background: A character's dialogue should reflect their education, upbringing, and personality.
- Example: Hagrid's rustic speech contrasts with Dumbledore's eloquence in Harry Potter.
- Use Subtext: What's left unsaid often speaks louder than words.
- Example: The tension-filled dinner in Get Out, where polite words mask hostility.
- Distinguish Voices: Each character should have a distinct way of speaking, whether through vocabulary, tone, or rhythm.

AI Tool: AI can analyze dialogue consistency and suggest ways to make it sharper or more distinct.

6. Relationships That Challenge Characters
Relationships are essential for character growth. They reveal hidden traits, create tension, and enrich the story.
Exploring Relationships
- Conflicts and Alliances: Relationships should evolve as characters change.
- Example: Woody and Buzz in Toy Story, who start as rivals but grow into partners.
- Power Dynamics: Relationships often involve shifting control.
- Example: Hannibal Lecter and Clarice Starling in The Silence of the Lambs.

7. Diversity and Representation
Writing diverse, authentic characters is essential in modern storytelling. Representation should be nuanced, not stereotypical.
Tips for Writing Diverse Characters
- Research Thoroughly: Understand cultures, experiences, and perspectives different from your own.
- Avoid Tokenism: Characters should have depth and purpose beyond their identity traits.
- Collaborate: Seek feedback from people with lived experiences.

AI Insight: AI tools can analyze for potential biases or suggest ways to deepen representation.

8. Writing Nontraditional Characters

Non-human or abstract characters can be just as compelling as human ones:

- WALL-E: A robot with human-like curiosity and love.
- Death in The Book Thief: An abstract narrator with a philosophical voice.

How to Relate Nontraditional Characters to Audiences:

- Give them human desires or emotions.
- Use body language or narration to convey their inner world.

9. How AI Can Enhance Character Development

- Character Profiling: Input a few traits, and AI can expand them into detailed profiles.
- Dialogue Refinement: AI can analyze tone, flow, and consistency across scenes.
- Archetype Blending: Combine traditional archetypes with unconventional traits.
- Simulating Interactions: Test how characters might behave in new situations.

10. Advanced Character Development Exercises

- Opposing Traits Exercise: Write a character with two conflicting traits (e.g., brave but superstitious).
- Character Journals: Write diary entries in the character's voice to explore their inner thoughts.
- Dialogue-Free Scene: Write a scene where the character's actions, not words, reveal their emotions and motivations.
- Simulate Growth: Use AI to explore how a character might change in response to different challenges.

11. Common Pitfalls and How to Avoid Them

- Flat Characters: Ensure every character has clear goals, motivations, and conflicts.
- Stereotypes: Avoid reducing characters to clichés.
- Unrealistic Dialogue: Focus on natural, distinct speech patterns.

Conclusion: Characters That Live Beyond the Screen

Characters breathe life into your screenplay. By understanding their psychology, relationships, and arcs, you can create individuals who resonate deeply with audiences. AI tools are powerful allies in this process, helping you refine and deepen your characters while preserving your unique creative vision.

Chapter 6: Emotional Resonance in Storytelling

Every great screenplay captures the audience's heart, evoking emotions that linger long after the credits roll. Whether it's the tearful joy of The Pursuit of Happyness, the adrenaline-fueled tension of The Dark Knight, or the bittersweet triumph in Inside Out, emotional resonance is what makes stories unforgettable. In this chapter, we'll explore how to craft stories that engage audiences emotionally. You'll learn to map emotional journeys, design impactful beats, balance tension and release, and use AI to analyze and refine your screenplay's emotional impact.

Why Emotional Resonance Matters
Emotional resonance transforms good stories into great ones. It's the connection that keeps audiences invested in the protagonist's journey, rooting for their success, and feeling their losses. It's also a key driver of a screenplay's marketability—producers know that emotionally compelling stories perform well with audiences and critics alike.

AI's Role:
AI doesn't replace emotional instinct but acts as a tool to enhance it. By analyzing emotional arcs and simulating audience responses, AI can help ensure your story delivers consistent and impactful emotional engagement.

1. Mapping Emotional Journeys
A screenplay isn't just a sequence of events—it's an emotional experience. Each story has an emotional arc that mirrors the protagonist's journey, building from setup to climax.
Emotional Beats in the Three-Act Structure:

Act 1: Establish the protagonist's emotional stakes.
  • Example: In Finding Nemo, Marlin's fear of losing his son establishes a clear emotional goal.

Act 2: Deepen emotional conflicts with rising tension.
  • Example: In Titanic, Jack and Rose's love story faces escalating threats, from social disapproval to the ship's sinking.

Act 3: Deliver an emotional payoff.
  • Example: In The Pursuit of Happyness, Chris Gardner's triumphant moment when he secures the job leaves audiences elated.

AI Application:
AI tools can create visual maps of your screenplay's emotional arc. If the emotional beats don't align with your story's structure, AI might suggest adjustments to enhance pacing or stakes.

2. Designing Key Emotional Beats
Certain moments in your screenplay will have the most significant emotional impact. These beats should be carefully crafted for maximum resonance.

Key Emotional Beats to Focus On:
- Inciting Incident: Create curiosity or shock to draw the audience in.
- Example: In Up, Carl meets Ellie as a child, setting up the emotional stakes for their love story.
- Midpoint: Introduce a major turning point or emotional revelation.
- Example: In The Lion King, Simba's encounter with Mufasa's ghost reignites his sense of purpose.
- Climax: Deliver the peak emotional payoff.
- Example: In The Dark Knight, Harvey Dent's transformation into Two-Face shocks both Bruce Wayne and the audience.

AI Application:
Use AI to analyze key beats for emotional engagement. For example, if your climax falls flat in simulated reactions, AI might suggest refining dialogue, stakes, or character decisions.

3. Balancing Tension and Release
Emotional pacing is critical to keeping your audience engaged. Too much tension can overwhelm, while too much downtime can bore.

Tension and Release Techniques:
- Alternate high-stakes scenes with quieter moments.
- Example: In Mad Max: Fury Road, brief pauses in action allow characters (and audiences) to process their emotions.
- Build tension gradually toward the climax.
- Example: In Parasite, the rising tension in the house party scene culminates in a shocking and chaotic resolution.

AI Application:
AI tools can analyze pacing to identify areas where tension overstays its welcome or quiet moments feel too prolonged. They might suggest condensing scenes or adding subplots to rebalance emotional flow.

4. Leveraging Subtext for Emotional Depth

Subtext is the unspoken emotional layer beneath dialogue and actions. It's what makes a scene resonate deeply with audiences.

Techniques for Using Subtext:
- Use visual metaphors to convey unspoken feelings.
- Example: In The Godfather, Michael closing the door on Kay symbolizes his complete separation from her.
- Create tension by letting the audience know more than the characters.
- Example: In Inglourious Basterds, the opening scene's subtext creates unbearable tension as we know the farmer is hiding Jews from Hans Landa.

Practical Exercise:
Write a scene heavy in subtext, such as a breakup where the characters never explicitly mention their feelings. Input it into an AI tool to analyze tone and suggest refinements.

5. Crafting Audience-Specific Emotional Journeys

Different audiences respond to different tones and themes. Tailor your emotional arc to match their expectations.

Examples of Audience-Specific Journeys:
- Family Dramas: Focus on warmth, reconciliation, and catharsis (The Pursuit of Happyness).
- Horror Films: Balance fear, dread, and relief (The Conjuring).
- Romantic Comedies: Build tension with misunderstandings, then deliver resolution (Crazy Rich Asians).

AI Insight:
AI can analyze your screenplay for tonal consistency and suggest adjustments to better align with your target demographic.

6. Practical Exercises

- Map Your Emotional Arc:
  - Choose a favorite film and identify its emotional beats. Then, map the beats of your screenplay to compare the emotional flow.
- Simulate Emotional Engagement:
  - Use AI to simulate audience reactions to your script. Focus on flagged moments where engagement dips, and revise scenes for greater emotional impact.
- Rewrite for Subtext:
  - Take a scene from your script and rewrite it with subtext in mind. Use AI to refine dialogue and ensure subtlety.

Conclusion: Emotional Resonance as the Heart of Storytelling
Emotion is the universal language of storytelling. It's what connects audiences to your characters, keeps them invested in the plot, and ensures your screenplay leaves a lasting impression. By mapping emotional journeys, designing key beats, and leveraging AI to refine your work, you can craft stories that resonate deeply with any audience.

Remember, AI is here to guide and enhance your instincts—not replace them. Your unique perspective and creativity are what will ultimately bring your screenplay to life.

Chapter 7: Subtext and Layers of Meaning

Great screenplays don't just tell a story—they imply, suggest, and resonate beyond the surface. Subtext is the art of conveying meaning without directly stating it, creating layers that engage the audience emotionally and intellectually. Mastering subtext allows your screenplay to speak volumes through subtlety, leaving a lasting impact.

In this chapter, we'll explore how to use subtext to add depth to your screenplay, analyze examples of subtext in action, and leverage AI to enhance subtlety in dialogue, scenes, and overarching narratives.

What is Subtext?
Subtext is the unspoken meaning beneath dialogue, actions, or visuals. It's the space between what is said and what is felt. Audiences connect with subtext because it allows them to actively engage with the story, filling in the gaps themselves.

Examples of Subtext in Screenplays:
- In The Godfather, Michael's cool demeanor during a heated argument conveys his shift toward becoming the family's enforcer.
- In Titanic, Rose's physical distance from Cal at the dinner table subtly reflects her emotional detachment.
- In Casablanca, Rick and Ilsa's dialogue about "Paris" carries layers of love, loss, and regret.

1. Types of Subtext
Understanding different types of subtext helps you apply them effectively in your screenplay:

A. Subtext in Dialogue
Dialogue often says one thing while meaning another.
- Example: In Inglourious Basterds, Hans Landa's polite tone masks his menacing intent.

AI Application: Input dialogue into an AI tool to analyze tone and detect mismatched emotions, ensuring the subtext lands effectively.

B. Subtext in Actions
Characters' behaviors often reveal more than their words.
- Example: In Get Out, Chris's hesitation before shaking Dean's hand conveys his unease about meeting his girlfriend's family.

AI Application: Use AI to analyze whether a character's actions align with or contradict their stated goals, enhancing tension or subtlety.

C. Visual Subtext
Visual elements can carry meaning without dialogue or explanation.
- Example: In The Social Network, Mark Zuckerberg's solitary posture at the end reflects his isolation despite his success.

2. Crafting Subtext in Your Screenplay
A. Start with Character Motivations
Subtext stems from characters' desires, fears, and secrets.
- Exercise: Write a scene where a character lies to protect their secret, and convey the truth through their actions or tone.

B. Use Conflict and Tension
Subtext thrives in moments of unspoken tension.
- Example: In Marriage Story, Charlie and Nicole's calm discussion of logistics is underpinned by their unspoken pain over their divorce.

AI Application: Use AI tools to test how dialogue and scene pacing build tension, suggesting refinements for emotional impact.

3. Building Layers of Meaning
Subtext works best when it operates on multiple levels, enriching the audience's experience as they uncover hidden meanings.

A. Layering Themes
Ensure your screenplay's theme resonates through subtext in character actions, dialogue, and visual motifs.
- Example: In Parasite, the recurring motif of the floodwaters reflects the family's rising and falling fortunes.

B. Foreshadowing Through Subtext
Use subtext to subtly hint at future events.
- Example: In The Sixth Sense, characters avoid interacting with Malcolm, foreshadowing the twist that he's a ghost.

4. Using AI to Enhance Subtext
AI tools can identify areas where subtext is weak or missing, and offer suggestions for improvement:

A. Tone Analysis
AI can detect whether a character's dialogue tone matches the intended subtext.

- Example: If a character's line, "I'm fine," feels too neutral, AI might suggest alternative phrasing to convey hidden anger or sadness.

B. Scene Dynamics
Input a scene into an AI tool to evaluate whether the subtext is creating the desired tension or ambiguity.
- Example: AI might highlight where actions are too explicit, recommending subtle adjustments.

C. Iterative Refinement
Experiment with multiple versions of a scene, using AI to test how each variation impacts subtext and audience engagement.

5. Practical Exercises
- Dialogue Rewrite for Subtext:
  o Take a straightforward line of dialogue and rewrite it to imply more than it says.
  o Example: Replace "I'm scared" with "I don't think this is a good idea," while showing fear through the character's body language.
- Subtext in Actions:
  o Write a scene where a character's actions reveal their true intentions, even as their words contradict them.
  o Use AI to analyze whether the scene communicates the intended subtext.
- Visual Metaphors:
  o Add a recurring visual motif to your screenplay that reflects a theme or character arc.
  o Example: A wilting plant symbolizes a strained relationship.

Conclusion: Subtext as the Soul of Storytelling
Subtext is where your screenplay transcends the literal and becomes truly impactful. By mastering subtext in dialogue, actions, and visuals, you invite audiences to engage with your story on a deeper level. With the help of AI tools to refine and analyze your screenplay, you can ensure your subtext enhances emotional depth and narrative complexity.

Remember, subtext is about trust—trusting your audience to read between the lines and connect with the layers you've built.

Chapter 8: World-Building and Immersive Settings

World-building isn't just for fantasy or science fiction—it's essential for any screenplay, from a small-town drama to a sprawling intergalactic epic. An immersive setting grounds your story, gives it authenticity, and enhances the audience's emotional connection.

In this chapter, we'll explore how to craft rich, believable worlds and use AI tools to ensure consistency, creativity, and depth in your settings.

1. What Makes World-Building Effective?
World-building is more than creating a backdrop—it's about shaping a living, breathing environment that interacts with your characters and plot. Effective world-building:
- Reflects the theme of the story.
- Influences characters' actions and decisions.
- Creates a unique identity that distinguishes your screenplay.
Example:
- In Blade Runner, the dystopian Los Angeles reflects themes of humanity and isolation.
- In Pride and Prejudice, the rigid societal norms shape the characters' decisions and conflicts.

2. Key Elements of World-Building
A. Physical Environment
The geography, architecture, and physical details of your world should immerse the audience.
- Example: Mad Max: Fury Road uses the desolate desert to amplify the stakes of survival.
AI Application:
Use AI tools to generate detailed descriptions or refine environmental consistency.
- Example: Input a general idea (e.g., "a futuristic city") and receive options for design, such as vertical gardens, autonomous transit systems, or weather-controlled domes.

B. Culture and Social Structures
Your world's societal norms, traditions, and hierarchies influence how characters interact.
- Example: In The Hunger Games, the Capitol's decadence contrasts with the impoverished districts, highlighting class inequality.

AI Application:
AI can analyze cultural elements to ensure consistency and suggest unique details.
Example: Input a setting description like "a post-apocalyptic society" and refine it with AI suggestions, such as cultural rituals for survival or unique slang reflecting the world's history.

C. Technology and Rules of the World
Clearly establish what's possible and what's not in your world, particularly in genres like sci-fi or fantasy.
- Example: In Avatar, the advanced technology of the humans contrasts with the spiritual connection of the Na'vi to their environment.

AI Application:
AI can help you brainstorm innovative technologies or rules that differentiate your world.
- Example: If you're writing about space travel, AI might suggest unique propulsion methods or intergalactic legal systems.

D. Sensory Details
Engage the audience with vivid sensory details—what characters see, hear, smell, and feel.
- Example: Parasite uses the contrast between the luxurious Parks' home and the cramped, dim Kim family's apartment to highlight social disparity.

AI Application:
Use AI to refine descriptions by generating sensory-rich phrases or adjusting tone for maximum immersion.

3. Integrating World-Building Into the Story
World-building should never overwhelm your narrative. Instead, it should serve the story and characters.

A. Show, Don't Tell
Reveal details of your world naturally through dialogue, actions, and visuals.
- Example: In Children of Men, the chaotic and decaying world is shown through background details like propaganda posters and crumbling infrastructure.

B. Let the World Shape the Plot
The setting should influence the story's events and stakes.
- Example: In Jaws, the ocean is both the setting and the central threat driving the plot.

C. Use World-Building to Enhance Conflict
Unique settings can heighten tension and challenges for characters.
- Example: In Gravity, space itself becomes the antagonist, creating unrelenting conflict for the protagonist.

4. Using AI to Enhance World-Building
AI tools can provide valuable assistance in crafting immersive and consistent settings:

A. Idea Generation
Input a basic concept (e.g., "a city on the moon") and let AI generate options for culture, geography, and societal norms.

B. Consistency Checks
AI can flag inconsistencies in your world's rules or details, ensuring your screenplay feels cohesive.
- Example: If your post-apocalyptic world has advanced technology in one scene and primitive tools in another, AI can suggest revisions.

C. Visualization Tools
Some AI platforms can create concept art or maps based on your descriptions, helping you better visualize your world and share it with collaborators.

5. Practical Exercises
- Build a Culture:
    - Define a tradition, ritual, or event unique to your world.
    - Example: A celebration of resource-sharing in a post-apocalyptic community.
    - Use AI to refine the tradition and integrate it into a pivotal scene.
- Describe a Setting:
    - Write a description of your screenplay's primary setting. Focus on sensory details and atmosphere.
    - Use AI to enhance or rephrase your description for clarity and impact.
- Map World Rules:
    - List the rules of your world (e.g., technological limits, social hierarchies). Ensure they align with your story's themes.
    - Use AI to test for contradictions or suggest additional rules that deepen the world's complexity.

Conclusion: Crafting a World That Feels Real
World-building is a powerful tool for immersing audiences in your story. Whether your screenplay is set in a small suburban town or a galaxy far, far away, the details of your world should enrich the narrative, reflect the theme, and shape the characters' journeys. By leveraging AI tools to brainstorm, refine, and visualize your world, you can create settings that are not only memorable but also integral to your story's success.

Remember, a great world isn't one that overshadows the characters —it's one that brings their story to life.

Chapter 9: Advanced Genre Writing

Every genre has its unique conventions, tropes, and audience expectations. Mastering these elements allows you to innovate within a genre, subvert expectations, and create standout screenplays. Whether it's the tension of horror, the laughter of comedy, or the adrenaline of action, understanding genre is essential for success.

In this chapter, we'll dive into advanced techniques for writing in specific genres, explore how AI can analyze audience preferences, and show how to balance tradition with innovation.

1. Why Genre Matters
Genres guide audience expectations and provide a framework for storytelling. While some writers treat genre as a limitation, it's better seen as a tool for creativity.
The Role of Genre:
- Audience Connection: Genres attract specific audiences with shared expectations.
    o Example: Horror fans expect fear and tension, while comedy fans seek laughter and light-hearted moments.
- Marketability: Genre influences how your screenplay is pitched and marketed to producers.
AI Application:
AI tools can analyze scripts in your chosen genre to identify patterns, such as pacing, character archetypes, or thematic elements.

2. Exploring Genre Conventions
A. Comedy
Comedy relies on timing, subversion, and relatability.
- Key Techniques:
    o Use unexpected twists to surprise and delight audiences (The Hangover).
    o Create flawed but lovable characters (Parks and Recreation).
- AI Application:
- AI can help refine comedic timing by analyzing dialogue rhythm or testing humor across different demographics.

B. Horror
Horror thrives on fear, tension, and unpredictability.
- Key Techniques:
  - Build suspense through pacing and visual cues (Hereditary).
  - Use subtext to explore societal fears (Get Out).
- AI Application:
- AI can map tension in your screenplay, suggesting where to increase stakes or add jump scares.

C. Drama
Drama focuses on character-driven stories with emotional depth.
- Key Techniques:
  - Craft relatable conflicts and high emotional stakes (Manchester by the Sea).
  - Use subplots to add layers and complexity (The Godfather).
- AI Application:
- AI can analyze character arcs to ensure growth and consistency.

D. Sci-Fi and Fantasy
These genres build immersive worlds while exploring universal themes.
- Key Techniques:
  - Anchor fantastical elements with relatable characters (The Martian).
  - Establish clear rules for your world (The Lord of the Rings).
- AI Application:
- AI can help brainstorm futuristic technologies, magical systems, or cultural details.

E. Action
Action scripts rely on kinetic energy, high stakes, and visual storytelling.
- Key Techniques:
  - Create clear, goal-oriented sequences (Mad Max: Fury Road).
  - Balance action with character development (Die Hard).
- AI Application:
- AI can help choreograph action sequences or analyze pacing for optimal intensity.

3. Innovating Within Genres

Sticking too closely to conventions can make your screenplay feel predictable. Innovating within a genre allows you to stand out while still satisfying audience expectations.

Techniques for Innovation:

- Subvert Tropes: Flip traditional genre tropes to surprise the audience.
  - Example: Knives Out reinvents the classic whodunit format with humor and modern twists.
- Blend Genres: Combine elements from multiple genres to create something fresh.
  - Example: Shaun of the Dead mixes horror and comedy seamlessly.

AI Application:

AI can analyze how genre-blending scripts like Get Out or Guardians of the Galaxy balance conventions, suggesting ways to integrate multiple genres effectively.

4. Adapting to Audience Expectations

Different audiences have different preferences and thresholds for genre elements. Understanding your target audience helps tailor your screenplay to their tastes.

Examples of Audience Adaptation:

- Horror: Younger audiences may prefer fast-paced scares, while older audiences may appreciate slow-burn psychological tension.
- Comedy: Cultural references may land differently depending on the demographic.

AI Application:

AI tools can simulate audience reactions based on age, region, or cultural preferences, helping you fine-tune your script.

5. Using AI to Master Genre Writing

AI tools offer several advantages when writing for specific genres:

- Genre Analysis: Input your script to compare its structure and tone to successful scripts in the same genre.
- Pacing Feedback: Analyze whether your screenplay maintains appropriate pacing for the genre.
- Idea Generation: Brainstorm unique concepts or twists within genre conventions.

6. Practical Exercises
- Analyze a Genre:
  - Choose a favorite film in your genre and break down its key conventions (e.g., pacing, character archetypes).
  - Map how your screenplay aligns with or subverts these conventions.
- Genre Blending Experiment:
  - Take two genres and combine their elements to write a short scene.
  - Example: A rom-com set during a zombie apocalypse.
- Simulate Audience Reactions:
  - Use an AI tool to analyze how your screenplay fits your chosen genre's expectations.
  - Revise sections flagged as too generic or predictable.

Conclusion: Elevating Your Genre Screenplay
Writing for a specific genre doesn't mean you're confined to a formula. Instead, genre provides a framework to build upon, offering opportunities to surprise, delight, or terrify your audience. By mastering conventions, blending elements, and leveraging AI for analysis and refinement, you can craft a screenplay that stands out while delivering exactly what your audience craves.

Chapter 10: Conflict and Resolution

Conflict drives every great story, and resolution gives it meaning. Without conflict, there's no tension to engage audiences, and without resolution, there's no payoff to satisfy them. In this chapter, we'll explore how to craft multi-layered conflicts, build compelling resolutions, and use AI to enhance the emotional and narrative impact of both.

1. The Role of Conflict in Storytelling
Conflict is the heart of storytelling, forcing characters to grow and adapt. It creates stakes, propels the plot, and keeps the audience invested.
Types of Conflict:
- Internal Conflict: The struggle within a character, often tied to their desires, fears, or values.
- Example: In Black Swan, Nina's ambition clashes with her psychological fragility.
- Interpersonal Conflict: The clash between characters.
- Example: The rivalry between Tony Stark and Steve Rogers in Captain America: Civil War.
- External Conflict: The challenges posed by the world or circumstances.
- Example: The survival struggle in The Revenant.

AI Application:
AI can help map the layers of conflict in your screenplay, identifying underdeveloped or redundant clashes.

2. Building Multi-Layered Conflicts
Layered conflicts create depth, engaging the audience on multiple levels.

A. Combining Conflict Types
Mix internal, interpersonal, and external conflicts to create a rich narrative.
- Example: In The Dark Knight, Batman faces internal doubts, clashes with Harvey Dent, and battles the Joker's chaotic schemes.

B. Escalating Conflict
Conflicts should intensify as the story progresses, culminating in the climax.
- Example: In Jurassic Park, the initial wonder of the dinosaurs escalates into a life-and-death struggle as the park's systems fail.

AI Application:
AI can identify points where conflict stagnates and suggest ways to raise stakes or increase tension.

3. Designing Compelling Resolutions
A strong resolution ties up your story's conflicts in a satisfying way, leaving the audience emotionally fulfilled.

A. Resolving Internal Conflict
The protagonist's personal growth should reflect their resolution of internal struggles.
- Example: In La La Land, Mia and Sebastian accept that their dreams have taken them in different directions, resolving their romantic conflict.

B. Delivering External Payoff
The climax should resolve external conflicts in a way that aligns with the story's themes.
- Example: In The Lord of the Rings, Frodo's journey ends with the destruction of the One Ring, fulfilling his quest and the larger thematic arc of sacrifice and hope.

C. Leaving Room for Reflection
Ambiguous or bittersweet resolutions can be powerful when they fit the story.
- Example: In Inception, the spinning top's ambiguity leaves the audience questioning reality alongside Cobb.

AI Application:
AI tools can analyze your resolution to ensure it aligns with the story's themes and emotional arcs, providing feedback on clarity and impact.

4. Conflict and Resolution Across Genres
Different genres handle conflict and resolution in unique ways. Understanding these nuances ensures your screenplay resonates with your target audience.
Examples:
- Horror: The resolution often leaves lingering fear, even if the immediate conflict is resolved (The Babadook).
- Romance: The resolution usually focuses on emotional closure and connection (When Harry Met Sally).
- Thriller: Resolutions tie up intricate plot threads while delivering a final twist (Se7en).

5. Using AI to Enhance Conflict and Resolution

AI tools can provide valuable insights at every stage of crafting conflict and resolution:

- Conflict Layering: Input character dynamics to identify opportunities for additional tension.
- Conflict Escalation: Analyze pacing to ensure conflicts build naturally toward the climax.
- Resolution Feedback: Test audience responses to your resolution, ensuring it's impactful and satisfying.

6. Practical Exercises

- Conflict Mapping:
  - Identify internal, interpersonal, and external conflicts in your screenplay.
  - Use AI to visualize how these conflicts interact and escalate.
- Rewrite a Resolution:
  - Take the resolution of a favorite film and rewrite it to subvert expectations.
  - Use AI to test how audiences might respond to the new ending.
- Climactic Scene Analysis:
  - Write the climactic scene of your screenplay. Focus on resolving the primary conflict while leaving room for thematic reflection.
  - Use AI to analyze the pacing and emotional impact of the scene.

7. Integrating Subplots to Enrich Conflict and Resolution

Subplots are more than secondary stories—they're tools to deepen your main narrative, amplify conflict, and provide emotional layers. A well-crafted subplot can reinforce themes, challenge the protagonist, and create opportunities for resolution that feel earned and satisfying.

A. The Role of Subplots in Conflict
Subplots should interact with the main plot, either by:
1. Mirroring the Main Conflict:
2. A subplot that reflects the primary conflict can highlight its stakes or themes.
   - Example: In The Dark Knight, Harvey Dent's descent mirrors Bruce Wayne's internal struggle with morality and responsibility.
3. Complicating the Main Plot:

4. A subplot can introduce obstacles or raise stakes for the protagonist.
   - Example: In The Hunger Games, Katniss's alliance with Rue complicates her survival by adding emotional stakes to the brutal competition.
5. Providing Contrast or Relief:
6. Subplots can create tonal shifts, offering moments of levity or reflection.
   - Example: In Lord of the Rings: The Two Towers, Merry and Pippin's interactions with Treebeard provide a break from the intense battles and emotional stakes of Frodo's journey.

B. The Role of Subplots in Resolution

Subplots can resolve independently or converge with the main plot, contributing to a layered and satisfying ending.
1. Subplots That Echo the Main Resolution:
2. When a subplot's resolution mirrors the main plot's themes, it reinforces the story's emotional impact.
   - Example: In Parasite, the subplot involving the housekeeper and her husband parallels the main family's desperation, leading to a climactic convergence.
3. Subplots That Introduce New Layers:
4. A subplot can leave the audience with questions or future possibilities, adding depth to the resolution.
   - Example: In Inception, the subplot of Cobb's guilt over his wife's death feeds directly into the ambiguous ending, leaving viewers with lingering emotional and thematic questions.

C. Using AI to Manage Subplots

AI tools can help track the interplay of subplots and the main plot, ensuring balance and consistency:
1. Mapping Subplot Arcs:
2. Input your subplot summaries into an AI tool to visualize how they align with the main narrative.
   - Example: AI might suggest connecting a secondary character's arc more directly to the protagonist's journey.
3. Analyzing Pacing:
4. Use AI to flag moments where subplots detract from the pacing of the main plot.
   - Example: If a subplot resolves too early, AI might recommend weaving it back into the climax.
5. Ensuring Thematic Alignment:
6. AI can identify whether subplots reinforce or detract from the screenplay's central theme, suggesting adjustments for cohesion.

D. Practical Exercise: Subplot Integration
- Outline Subplots:
  - Write a one-paragraph summary for each subplot in your screenplay.
  - Identify how each subplot interacts with the main plot (e.g., mirroring, complicating, contrasting).
- Align Subplot Beats:
  - Place key subplot moments on a timeline alongside the main plot.
  - Ensure subplots escalate tension or deepen themes without distracting from the primary narrative.
- AI Review:
  - Input your timeline into an AI tool to analyze pacing, thematic alignment, and character dynamics.
  - Revise subplot scenes based on AI suggestions to enhance their connection to the main plot.

Subplots are powerful tools that can enrich your screenplay's conflict and resolution, creating a multidimensional narrative that resonates with audiences. By aligning subplots with the main story, escalating tension, and using AI to ensure balance and cohesion, you can elevate your screenplay from engaging to unforgettable.

Conclusion: The Art of Conflict and Resolution
Conflict gives your story its beating heart, while resolution gives it purpose. By layering conflicts, escalating tension, and delivering meaningful resolutions, you create a screenplay that resonates deeply with audiences. With the help of AI tools, you can refine these elements to ensure your story is as engaging and impactful as possible.

Remember, conflict isn't just about action—it's about transformation. And resolution isn't just about closure—it's about leaving your audience with something to think about, long after the credits roll.

Chapter 11: Writing for Episodic and Streaming Media

The rise of streaming platforms and episodic storytelling has transformed the screenwriting landscape. Writers must now adapt their stories to fit bingeable formats, episodic arcs, and audience expectations for long-form storytelling. Whether crafting a multi-season epic or a self-contained limited series, understanding the nuances of episodic media is essential.

This chapter explores how to structure episodic narratives, design engaging arcs, and use AI to refine scripts for TV shows, web series, and other streaming formats.

1. The Fundamentals of Episodic Storytelling
Episodic writing differs from feature-length screenwriting in several ways. Instead of one story arc, you're crafting multiple, interconnected arcs that unfold across episodes or seasons.

Key Elements of Episodic Storytelling:
- Episode Arcs: Each episode must have its own mini-story that resolves or progresses while feeding into the larger narrative.
  - Example: In Breaking Bad, each episode builds Walter White's transformation while resolving smaller conflicts.
- Season Arcs: The season as a whole must follow a larger, cohesive arc.
  - Example: In Stranger Things, the kids' investigation of Will's disappearance drives the first season's central story.
- Series Arcs: Multi-season shows require overarching themes and conflicts to keep audiences invested.
  - Example: In Game of Thrones, the battle for the Iron Throne spans the entire series.

AI Application:
AI tools can map episode beats and season arcs, identifying inconsistencies or underdeveloped threads.

2. Structuring Episodic Narratives
A. Balancing Episodic and Serial Elements
Episodic storytelling combines self-contained episodes with overarching serial narratives.
- Example: The X-Files balances "monster of the week" episodes with the larger conspiracy plot.

AI Application:
Input your episodic structure into an AI tool to visualize the balance between episodic and serial elements, ensuring audience engagement.

B. Crafting Bingeable Content
Streaming platforms thrive on bingeable shows that encourage viewers to watch multiple episodes in one sitting.
- Key Techniques:
  - End episodes with a "hook" or cliffhanger to propel viewers into the next episode.
  - Example: The Mandalorian often ends episodes with a new challenge or mystery.
  - Maintain consistent pacing to avoid lulls.

AI Application:
Use AI to analyze pacing across episodes, identifying areas where momentum dips and suggesting adjustments.

3. Designing Compelling Characters for Episodic Media
Characters in episodic storytelling must sustain interest over multiple episodes or seasons. This requires depth, relatability, and growth.
A. Character Arcs in Episodic Formats
- Short-Term Growth: Minor changes occur within an episode.
  - Example: In The Office, Jim and Dwight's rivalry often resolves temporarily by the episode's end.
- Long-Term Growth: Character arcs evolve over a season or series.
  - Example: In The Crown, Queen Elizabeth's role as monarch is explored in-depth over multiple seasons.

AI Application:
AI can analyze character arcs to ensure they align with episodic and serial storytelling demands.

B. Ensemble Casts and Subplots
Episodic storytelling often features ensemble casts, allowing for multiple subplots and perspectives.
- Example: Orange Is the New Black explores various inmates' stories while maintaining Piper's central arc.

AI Application:
Use AI to track subplots and ensure they contribute to the main narrative without overwhelming it.

4. Navigating Streaming-Specific Challenges
A. Audience Data and Retention
Streaming platforms rely on data-driven insights to understand audience preferences.
- Example: Netflix analyzes viewership patterns to inform pacing and hook placement.

AI Application:
AI tools can simulate audience reactions and suggest edits to improve engagement at critical moments.

B. Adapting to Platform Requirements
Each streaming platform has unique preferences for format, tone, and content.
- Example: HBO leans toward darker, prestige dramas, while Disney+ emphasizes family-friendly adventure.

Practical Tip: Research your target platform and tailor your script to fit its style.

5. Practical Exercises
- Map Your Season Arc:
  - Write a one-paragraph summary of your season's main storyline.
  - Break the story into episodic beats, ensuring each episode contributes to the overall arc.
  - Use AI to analyze the flow and suggest adjustments for pacing or engagement.
- Write a Cliffhanger Scene:
  - Write the final scene of an episode, ending on a compelling hook or mystery.
  - Test it with AI to ensure it builds excitement and curiosity for the next episode.
- Analyze an Ensemble Cast:
  - Choose an ensemble show and map how subplots interact with the main storyline.
  - Apply these techniques to your script, ensuring balance and integration.

Conclusion: The Art of Episodic Storytelling
Episodic and streaming formats demand a unique approach to screenwriting, blending self-contained episodes with overarching narratives. By mastering episodic structure, creating bingeable arcs, and leveraging AI to refine pacing and character dynamics, you can craft stories that resonate with modern audiences.

Remember, every episode is a chapter in a larger story—ensure each one leaves viewers eager for the next.

Chapter 12: Interactive and Participatory Storytelling

The rise of interactive media has revolutionized storytelling. From choose-your-own-adventure narratives to immersive VR experiences, modern audiences want to engage directly with stories, influencing outcomes and exploring multiple paths. Writing for interactive formats like video games, virtual reality (VR), augmented reality (AR), and interactive films requires a unique approach that balances freedom with narrative coherence.

This chapter explores how to craft branching narratives, design player or audience agency, and use AI to manage the complexities of interactive storytelling.

1. Understanding Interactive Storytelling
Interactive storytelling invites the audience to influence the narrative through their decisions or actions. Unlike traditional formats, interactive stories must account for multiple possible outcomes while maintaining emotional engagement.

Key Features of Interactive Storytelling:
- Branching Narratives: Stories that split into multiple paths based on audience choices.
    - Example: Black Mirror: Bandersnatch allows viewers to make decisions that shape the story's outcome.
- Player Agency: The degree of control given to the audience over characters or plot points.
    - Example: In The Witcher 3, players' choices impact relationships and world events.
- Replayability: Interactive stories often encourage revisiting to explore different paths.

AI Application:
AI can assist in planning branching narratives, ensuring each path feels meaningful and cohesive.

2. Crafting Branching Narratives
Branching narratives require careful planning to ensure that every path is compelling, logical, and aligned with the story's themes.

A. Decision Points
Identify key moments where the audience can influence the story.
- Example: In Detroit: Become Human, players make moral and strategic decisions that affect character fates and endings.

AI Application:
AI can help identify decision points that maximize emotional impact and engagement, suggesting alternate outcomes based on audience preferences.

B. Designing Outcomes
Each choice should lead to meaningful consequences, reinforcing the audience's sense of agency.
- Example: In Life Is Strange, players' choices ripple across episodes, shaping relationships and events.

AI Application:
AI can simulate audience responses to different outcomes, ensuring each feels satisfying and impactful.

C. Maintaining Narrative Cohesion
Branching narratives must remain consistent, even as they diverge.
- Techniques:
    - Use recurring themes or motifs to tie branches together.
    - Design "merge points" where separate paths converge back into the main story.
- Example: In Until Dawn, character relationships and plotlines evolve based on choices, but all branches align with the story's central themes of survival and trust.

3. Designing Immersive Interactive Experiences
Interactive storytelling often extends beyond traditional screenwriting into immersive formats like VR and AR.

A. Writing for Virtual Reality
VR storytelling immerses the audience in a 360-degree environment where they are active participants.
- Example: The Invisible Hours places viewers inside a murder mystery, allowing them to explore the story from different perspectives.

Tips for VR Storytelling:
- Create environments rich in detail to reward exploration.
- Use subtle cues to guide the audience without breaking immersion.

B. Writing for Games
Video games combine storytelling with gameplay, requiring a balance between narrative depth and player freedom.
- Example: Red Dead Redemption 2 seamlessly integrates an emotional story with open-world gameplay.

AI Application:
AI can help design branching dialogues, non-player character (NPC) behaviors, and dynamic storytelling elements.

4. The Role of AI in Interactive Storytelling
AI is invaluable for managing the complexity of interactive narratives, offering tools for planning, testing, and refining:

A. Mapping Narrative Paths
AI can visualize branching narratives, ensuring every path is cohesive and aligned with the story's goals.

B. Simulating Player Choices
AI can predict audience preferences and simulate how different choices impact engagement and emotional resonance.

C. Refining Replayability
AI can suggest tweaks to encourage replayability by highlighting underused paths or enhancing overlooked outcomes.

5. Practical Exercises
- Create a Branching Narrative Map:
  - Choose a key decision point in your screenplay. Write at least three possible outcomes, ensuring each aligns with the story's theme.
  - Use AI to test how these paths impact pacing and engagement.
- Write an Immersive VR Scene:
  - Describe a 360-degree environment where the audience can freely explore. Include details that reveal the story through interactions.
  - Use AI to refine descriptions and ensure logical flow.
- Simulate Audience Choices:
  - Input a branching scene into an AI tool and analyze predicted audience responses. Adjust the scene to maximize emotional impact.

Conclusion: Engaging Audiences Through Interactivity
Interactive storytelling offers limitless creative possibilities, empowering audiences to shape their own experiences. By mastering branching narratives, designing immersive environments, and leveraging AI to manage complexity, you can craft stories that captivate and engage in entirely new ways.

Remember, interactive storytelling isn't about relinquishing control —it's about guiding your audience through an experience that feels uniquely their own.

Chapter 13: Writing for Global and Cross-Cultural Audiences

In today's interconnected world, screenwriters must think beyond borders. Audiences on streaming platforms come from diverse cultural backgrounds, and stories that resonate globally often find the most success. Writing for a global audience requires cultural sensitivity, an understanding of universal themes, and the ability to adapt storytelling for international appeal.

This chapter explores techniques for creating cross-cultural narratives, tailoring stories for global audiences, and using AI to analyze and refine scripts for cultural relevance.

1. Why Write for a Global Audience?
Global storytelling offers opportunities to reach broader markets, build universal appeal, and create stories that transcend cultural barriers.

Benefits of Writing for a Global Audience:
- Expanded Reach: Streaming platforms like Netflix, Amazon Prime, and Disney+ cater to international audiences.
- Cultural Universality: Stories with universal themes (e.g., love, sacrifice, resilience) connect across cultural boundaries.
  - Example: Parasite explored class disparity in a South Korean setting but resonated worldwide due to its universal theme.
- Diverse Perspectives: Incorporating multiple cultural perspectives enriches storytelling and offers fresh viewpoints.

2. Building Cross-Cultural Stories
A. Start with Universal Themes
Themes like family, justice, or survival resonate globally while allowing for cultural specificity.
- Example: Coco celebrates Mexican culture while exploring universal themes of family and remembrance.

B. Incorporate Specific Cultural Details
Rich cultural details make stories authentic and relatable.
- Example: Slumdog Millionaire combines universal themes of love and perseverance with a deeply Indian cultural backdrop.

C. Respect Cultural Sensitivities
Avoid stereotypes, tokenism, or inaccuracies by conducting thorough research.

- Example: Black Panther showcases African-inspired designs and traditions without reducing them to clichés.

AI Application:
AI tools can flag potential cultural insensitivities or suggest ways to enrich cultural details.

3. Tailoring Stories for Global Markets
Different markets have unique storytelling preferences. Adapting your screenplay for these preferences can maximize its appeal.

A. Regional Tropes and Expectations
Understand the tropes and conventions that resonate in specific regions.
- Example: Asian audiences often favor family-centric dramas, while Western audiences lean toward individual heroism.

AI Application:
Use AI to analyze successful films in specific markets and identify patterns in tone, structure, or character dynamics.

B. Multilingual Accessibility
Global audiences may experience your screenplay in translated or dubbed formats. Writing with this in mind can improve accessibility.
- Example: Avoid puns or idioms that may not translate well.

AI Application:
AI can analyze dialogue for translation challenges or suggest alternatives that maintain meaning across languages.

C. Localization vs. Universality
Striking the right balance between universal appeal and cultural specificity is key.
- Example: Minari is a deeply Korean-American story, but its themes of family and perseverance resonate universally.

4. Using AI to Write for Global Audiences
AI tools can assist in crafting culturally relevant and globally resonant stories in several ways:

A. Cultural Sensitivity Analysis
AI can flag stereotypes, clichés, or inaccuracies that may alienate audiences.

B. Global Audience Testing
Simulate audience reactions in different regions to gauge how your screenplay might be received.
- Example: AI might suggest emphasizing certain plot points for better reception in European markets.

C. Language Optimization
AI can suggest dialogue adjustments for easier translation or highlight potential localization issues.

5. Practical Exercises
- Identify Universal Themes:
  - Write a one-paragraph summary of your screenplay's theme. Highlight how it connects to global audiences.
  - Use AI to test how the theme resonates across different cultural demographics.
- Incorporate Cultural Details:
  - Research a specific cultural setting for your screenplay. Write a scene that incorporates local traditions, values, or language.
  - Use AI to refine the scene for authenticity and cultural sensitivity.
- Simulate Global Audience Reactions:
  - Input your screenplay into an AI tool to analyze how different markets might respond to tone, dialogue, or themes. Adjust based on feedback.

Conclusion: Crafting Stories for the World
Writing for a global audience is both an opportunity and a responsibility. By balancing universal themes with cultural specificity, you can create stories that resonate across borders. With AI as your ally, you can ensure your screenplay is culturally sensitive, universally appealing, and ready to captivate audiences worldwide.

Remember, great stories transcend boundaries—they bring people together by celebrating our shared humanity.

Chapter 14: Scene Construction and Visual Storytelling

A screenplay lives and dies by its scenes. They are the foundation of your story, and each one must serve a purpose, advance the narrative, and captivate the audience visually and emotionally. By learning to craft dynamic scenes and harness the power of visual storytelling, you can elevate your screenplay into something truly cinematic.

In this expanded chapter, we'll explore scene construction through detailed examples from iconic films, analyze how visual storytelling enhances the narrative, and show how AI tools can refine these elements to create compelling screenplays.

1. The Fundamentals of Scene Construction
A scene should always do at least one of the following:
1. Advance the plot.
2. Reveal or develop character.
3. Establish tone or theme.
Let's analyze these elements through examples:

A. Advancing the Plot
- Example: The Restaurant Scene from The Godfather
- Michael's decision to kill Sollozzo and the police captain moves the story forward by cementing his transformation from reluctant outsider to ruthless heir of the Corleone family.
  - Why It Works: The scene has a clear objective (Michael must decide to kill), escalating tension (waiting for the gun in the bathroom), and a resolution (Michael's decisive action).

Practical Exercise:
Choose a pivotal scene in your screenplay. Write down its purpose in one sentence. If it doesn't advance the plot, rewrite it to include a decision, discovery, or action that changes the story's direction.

B. Revealing or Developing Character
- Example: The "Royale with Cheese" Scene from Pulp Fiction
- Jules and Vincent's casual conversation about European McDonald's reveals their personalities, their relationship, and sets up the juxtaposition of mundane banter with the violence that follows.
  - Why It Works: The dialogue humanizes the characters while subtly establishing their camaraderie before the action.

Practical Exercise:
Rewrite a scene in your screenplay to reveal a key trait about your character using dialogue, actions, or choices. Use AI tools to analyze whether these traits are consistently reflected throughout your script.

C. Establishing Tone or Theme
- Example: The Opening Scene from The Dark Knight
- The bank heist introduces the Joker, his chaotic methods, and the theme of escalation in Gotham's criminal underworld.
  - Why It Works: Every action in the scene builds toward the Joker's climactic reveal, immersing the audience in the film's tone of calculated chaos.

AI Application:
Use AI to analyze whether your scenes consistently match your screenplay's tone or deviate unintentionally.

2. Visual Storytelling: Show, Don't Tell
A. Leveraging Visual Metaphors
Visual metaphors convey themes and emotions without explicit exposition.
- Example: The Red Coat in Schindler's List
- The girl's red coat amidst a monochrome world symbolizes innocence lost in the Holocaust, creating a haunting visual impact.
  - Why It Works: The metaphor is subtle yet powerful, staying with the audience long after the scene ends.

Practical Exercise:
Identify a theme in your screenplay and brainstorm a visual metaphor that can represent it. Rewrite a scene to integrate this metaphor organically.

B. Framing and Composition
The way a scene is framed influences audience perception.
- Example: The Overhead Shot in The Shining
- The maze sequence uses a bird's-eye view to emphasize Jack's isolation and the labyrinthine nature of his mind.
  - Why It Works: The composition reinforces the psychological terror of the scene.

Practical Exercise:
Write descriptions for how you'd frame a key scene in your screenplay. Use AI-powered visualization tools to test whether your framing enhances the intended emotional impact.

C. Actions Speak Louder Than Words
- Example: The Wordless Opening of Wall-E
- The robot's lonely routines on a desolate Earth speak volumes about his longing for connection.
    - Why It Works: The lack of dialogue forces the audience to focus on Wall-E's actions and environment, creating empathy through visuals alone.

Practical Exercise:
Rewrite a dialogue-heavy scene from your screenplay as a purely visual sequence. Use AI to analyze whether the revised scene maintains emotional clarity.

3. Crafting Scene Openings and Closures
A. Scene Openings
A strong opening grabs the audience's attention immediately.
- Example: The Diner Scene from Reservoir Dogs
- The characters' casual conversation about tipping sets the tone for the film while introducing key personalities.
    - Why It Works: The mundane topic contrasts sharply with the criminal world they inhabit, hooking the audience with intrigue.

B. Scene Closures
An impactful closure leaves the audience eager for what's next.
- Example: The Spinning Top in Inception
- The unresolved question of whether Cobb is in reality or a dream creates lasting engagement.
    - Why It Works: Ambiguity encourages viewers to reflect on the story, extending its emotional resonance.

AI Application:
Analyze scene openings and closures for their ability to grab attention and maintain engagement.

4. Building Emotional Beats Through Visuals

A. Use of Lighting and Color

Lighting and color amplify emotion and theme.

- Example: Neon Lighting in Drive
- The film's neon palette reflects the protagonist's dual nature—romantic by day, violent by night.
  - Why It Works: The visual style reinforces the tension between beauty and brutality.

Practical Exercise:

Choose a key scene and rewrite its description, focusing on how lighting and color can emphasize mood and theme.

B. Silent Tension

- Example: The Silence in No Country for Old Men
- The hotel confrontation between Llewelyn and Chigurh uses silence and stillness to create unbearable tension.
  - Why It Works: Silence forces the audience to focus on the characters' subtle movements and the ticking clock of inevitability.

Practical Exercise:

Write a scene where silence heightens tension. Use AI to ensure pacing and emotional beats are balanced.

5. Using AI to Enhance Scene Construction

AI tools can elevate your scene construction and visual storytelling:

- Previsualization Tools: Generate concept art or basic animations to visualize complex scenes.
- Tone Consistency Analysis: Ensure every scene aligns with the screenplay's intended tone.
- Conflict Mapping: Test how each scene's conflict builds toward the climax.

6. Expanded Practical Exercises
- Analyze a Famous Scene:
  - Choose a scene from a favorite film (e.g., the restaurant scene in The Godfather). Break it down into purpose, conflict, and resolution.
  - Apply the same framework to one of your scenes.
- Storyboard Key Moments:
  - Write descriptions of camera angles, lighting, and visual metaphors for a pivotal scene.
  - Use AI previsualization to test the effectiveness of your storyboard.
- Rewrite for Visual Impact:
  - Take a dialogue-heavy scene and rewrite it to rely solely on actions, framing, and subtext.
  - Use AI to compare audience engagement for both versions.

Conclusion: Mastering Scene Construction and Visual Storytelling
A compelling scene doesn't just tell a story—it immerses the audience in its world, evokes emotions, and leaves a lasting impact. By learning from iconic examples, focusing on visual storytelling, and leveraging AI to refine your work, you can craft scenes that resonate deeply with your audience.

Remember, every scene is an opportunity to captivate. Make each one count.

Chapter 15: Dialogue That Resonates

Dialogue is the heartbeat of a screenplay. It reveals character, conveys conflict, drives the story, and keeps the audience engaged. But great dialogue is more than just words—it's rhythm, subtext, and emotion. Every line should serve a purpose, from advancing the plot to building tension or delivering humor.

In this chapter, we'll explore how to craft memorable, authentic, and impactful dialogue. Drawing on examples from famous scripts, we'll analyze what makes dialogue effective and how to use AI to refine your writing.

1. The Purpose of Dialogue
Dialogue in screenwriting serves three main purposes:
1. Revealing Character: Dialogue should reflect who your characters are—their motivations, values, and emotional states.
2. Driving the Plot: Dialogue moves the story forward, providing exposition, raising stakes, or escalating conflict.
3. Adding Subtext: The best dialogue often says one thing while meaning another, creating depth and engagement.

A. Revealing Character
- Example: Jules in Pulp Fiction
- Jules's speech about "divine intervention" after surviving a shootout reveals his deep conflict and sets up his character's transformation.
   - Why It Works: His dialogue balances humor, introspection, and tension, making him complex and relatable.

B. Driving the Plot
- Example: The Interrogation in The Dark Knight
- The Joker's taunts during his confrontation with Batman drive the narrative by revealing his plan to corrupt Harvey Dent.
   - Why It Works: The dialogue builds tension and forces Batman to confront moral dilemmas, escalating the stakes.

C. Adding Subtext
- Example: The Dinner Table Scene in Get Out
- The Armitage family's seemingly friendly questions carry sinister undertones, foreshadowing their true intentions.
   - Why It Works: The dialogue's subtext builds unease while maintaining a veneer of civility.

2. Characteristics of Great Dialogue
A. Authenticity
Great dialogue feels real but is never mundane. It reflects how people speak while cutting unnecessary filler.
- Example: The "Royale with Cheese" Scene in Pulp Fiction
- Jules and Vincent's casual conversation feels authentic but is carefully crafted to reveal their relationship and worldview.
  - Why It Works: The dialogue combines humor with character insights, grounding the audience in their dynamic.

B. Economy
Every word of dialogue should serve a purpose, either advancing the plot or deepening character.
- Example: Quint's Monologue in Jaws
- Quint's brief yet haunting story about the USS Indianapolis not only reveals his motivations but also builds tension for the shark hunt.
  - Why It Works: The monologue conveys exposition, emotion, and stakes without feeling bloated.

C. Rhythm and Flow
Dialogue has a natural rhythm that keeps the audience engaged. This includes pacing, pauses, and interruptions.
- Example: The Coffee Shop Scene in Heat
- The back-and-forth between Pacino and De Niro showcases their mutual respect and clashing ideologies.
  - Why It Works: The dialogue's rhythm mirrors the characters' psychological chess match, maintaining tension despite its calm setting.

3. Writing Dialogue for Different Genres
A. Comedy
Comedy thrives on timing, wordplay, and irony.
- Example: Ghostbusters
- Venkman's quips lighten the supernatural stakes while reinforcing his irreverent personality.
  - Why It Works: The humor adds levity without undermining the tension.

B. Drama
Drama relies on dialogue to explore character relationships and conflicts.
- Example: Marriage Story
- The argument between Charlie and Nicole is raw and unfiltered, exposing their vulnerabilities.
  - Why It Works: The dialogue feels authentic, emotionally charged, and deeply personal.

C. Thriller
Thrillers use dialogue to build suspense and misdirect the audience.
- Example: No Country for Old Men
- Chigurh's conversation with the gas station attendant turns a mundane interaction into a nerve-wracking scene.
  - Why It Works: The dialogue's subtext creates an atmosphere of unpredictability and dread.

4. Leveraging Subtext in Dialogue
Subtext is the art of saying one thing while meaning another. It adds depth and engages the audience by requiring them to infer the true meaning.

- Example: The Final Scene in Casablanca
- Rick's farewell to Ilsa—"Here's looking at you, kid"—conveys his love and sacrifice without explicitly stating it.
  - Why It Works: The dialogue leaves room for interpretation, making it more emotionally impactful.

Practical Exercise:
Write a dialogue-heavy scene where the characters' words contradict their actions. Use AI to analyze tone and suggest refinements for clarity and subtlety.

5. Using AI to Refine Dialogue
AI tools can assist in crafting and polishing dialogue in several ways:

- Analyzing Tone Consistency: AI can ensure your characters' dialogue stays true to their personalities and emotional arcs.
- Enhancing Subtext: Input dialogue to identify where subtext can be added or improved.
- Optimizing Rhythm and Flow: AI tools can analyze pacing and suggest edits to improve naturalism.

Example: Use AI to test multiple variations of a critical conversation, identifying which version resonates most with the intended emotional tone.

6. Practical Exercises
- Rewrite with Subtext:
  - Take a straightforward exchange from your script and rewrite it to imply, rather than state, the characters' feelings.
  - Test with AI to ensure the subtext is clear.
- Analyze Famous Dialogue:
  - Choose a memorable line from a favorite film. Break it down: What does it reveal about the character? How does it advance the story?
  - Apply the same principles to a scene in your screenplay.
- Dialogue Economy Challenge:
  - Take a long conversation in your script and cut it in half while retaining its meaning. Use AI to verify that nothing essential is lost.

Conclusion: The Art of Resonant Dialogue
Great dialogue is a blend of authenticity, purpose, and rhythm. By learning from iconic examples, mastering subtext, and leveraging AI to refine your writing, you can craft dialogue that resonates deeply with audiences.

Remember, the best dialogue doesn't just communicate—it captivates. Every word is an opportunity to reveal, engage, and leave a lasting impression.

Chapter 16: Sound and Music in Screenwriting

Sound and music are vital storytelling tools in filmmaking. They create mood, build tension, and evoke emotions in ways that dialogue and visuals alone cannot. While screenwriters may not directly compose scores or design soundscapes, understanding the role of sound and music can help you craft more immersive and impactful scripts. By thoughtfully incorporating cues and experimenting with modern tools, you can elevate your screenplay to a truly cinematic level.

This chapter explores the art and science of sound and music in storytelling, provides practical examples from iconic films, and introduces cutting-edge AI tools that enable writers to experiment with soundscapes and musical ideas.

The Role of Sound in Storytelling
Sound is the invisible thread that ties together atmosphere, emotion, and narrative. It can evoke tension, signify changes, or even serve as a character in its own right.
Sound as Atmosphere
Sound breathes life into a setting, grounding the audience in the story's world.
- Example: A Quiet Place
- The eerie silence punctuated by rustling leaves and distant footsteps immerses the audience in the film's rules, where every sound is a threat.
  - Why It Works: The silence becomes part of the story's tension, making every noise deliberate and terrifying.

Sound as a Narrative Device
Sound cues can signal plot shifts, foreshadow events, or reveal unseen forces.
- Example: The Sixth Sense
- A sudden, unsettling piano note underscores Malcolm's realization that something supernatural is happening.
  - Why It Works: The sound cue conveys a sense of foreboding, adding to the scene's emotional weight without dialogue.

The Power of Music in Film
Music is the emotional undercurrent of a screenplay. It enhances drama, signals shifts in tone, and creates unforgettable moments.
Using Music to Evoke Emotion

Music can transform a scene from mundane to extraordinary by aligning the score with the characters' emotional journey.
- Example: Rocky
- The iconic training montage set to "Gonna Fly Now" inspires hope and determination as Rocky prepares for his fight.
    - Why It Works: The music becomes synonymous with Rocky's resilience, amplifying the emotional payoff.

Leitmotifs and Recurring Themes
Recurring musical themes help reinforce character arcs or thematic elements.
- Example: Star Wars
- The "Imperial March" accompanies Darth Vader, signaling menace and authority.
    - Why It Works: Leitmotifs create emotional associations, making characters instantly recognizable through sound.

Juxtaposing Music and Action
Contrasting upbeat music with dark visuals can create unforgettable scenes.
- Example: Reservoir Dogs
- "Stuck in the Middle with You" plays as Mr. Blonde tortures a hostage, creating a disturbing juxtaposition.
    - Why It Works: The contrast heightens discomfort, leaving a lasting impression on the viewer.

Incorporating Sound and Music Cues Into Your Script
While screenwriters don't dictate the final score or sound design, strategic cues can guide directors and composers, ensuring your vision is understood.

Writing Subtle Sound Cues
Sound cues should be purposeful and sparingly used to avoid overloading the script.
- How to Write It:
    - "The faint sound of a ticking clock grows louder as tension builds in the room."

Suggesting Musical Tone
Focus on the tone of the music rather than specifying exact tracks.
- How to Write It:
    - "Somber strings swell as the protagonist gazes at the wreckage of their home."

Silence as a Choice
Sometimes, the absence of sound is more impactful than music or noise.
- Example: No Country for Old Men
- The film's lack of a traditional score amplifies its tension and stark realism.

The Rise of AI-Generated Sound and Music
With advancements in AI, writers can now experiment with soundscapes and musical ideas early in the creative process. AI tools enable screenwriters to hear how sound and music might complement their scenes, offering opportunities for innovation.

AI Tools for Sound and Music
- Suno.AI:
    - Generates custom musical scores and soundscapes tailored to the emotional tone of a scene.
    - Example: Input a description of your scene, such as "intense chase through a dark forest," and Suno.AI produces a fitting audio track.
- AIVA (Artificial Intelligence Virtual Artist):
    - Composes music based on script mood, allowing you to experiment with thematic leitmotifs.
- Boom Library AI Sound Tools:
    - Helps generate ambient sounds and effects like rain, footsteps, or cityscapes for immersive settings.

Experimenting With AI Sounds in Screenwriting
AI offers opportunities to test how soundscapes and music can enhance your script before production.

Practical Applications:
- Sound Design Simulations:
  - Use AI tools to create background sounds for a key scene, such as ocean waves, city noise, or wind in a haunted forest.
  - Play these while reading your scene to evaluate how they complement the mood.
- Dynamic Music Experiments:
  - Test multiple musical themes for a scene. For example, create a suspenseful track and a melancholic track to see which enhances the scene's tone better.
- Real-Time Feedback:
  - Use tools like Suno.AI to adjust pacing or tension in the music, ensuring alignment with the emotional beats of your screenplay.

Practical Exercises
- Create a Soundscape:
  - Write a description of a scene's ambient sounds (e.g., a bustling market, a desolate battlefield). Use AI to generate these sounds and play them as you refine your script.
- Rewrite for Musical Impact:
  - Choose a key moment in your screenplay. Suggest a musical tone that enhances the scene's emotion, and test AI-generated tracks to match the description.
- Experiment With Silence:
  - Rewrite a dialogue-heavy scene, replacing spoken lines with silence and sound cues. Evaluate the impact by playing a simulated soundscape.

Iconic Sound and Music Moments in Film
The Opening of Apocalypse Now
- Description: The whir of helicopter blades fades into The Doors' "The End" as napalm explodes across the jungle.
- Why It Works: The sound and music together establish the film's tone of chaos and psychological disarray.

The Shower Scene in Psycho
- Description: The shrieking violins mimic the stabbing motion, creating an iconic auditory representation of terror.
- Why It Works: The sound becomes inseparable from the visual, amplifying the horror.

The Ending of The Graduate
- Description: Simon & Garfunkel's "The Sound of Silence" underscores Benjamin and Elaine's uncertain expressions as they flee on a bus.
- Why It Works: The music reflects the bittersweet ambiguity of their decision, leaving a lasting impression.

Conclusion: Crafting the Sound of Your Story
Sound and music are indispensable tools for creating immersive and emotionally resonant screenplays. By understanding their role, incorporating thoughtful cues, and leveraging AI to experiment with soundscapes and themes, you can take your storytelling to the next level.

Remember, great sound and music don't just accompany the visuals—they amplify the story, transforming moments into memories.

Chapter 17: Breaking Into the Industry

Breaking into the screenwriting industry is a journey filled with challenges, perseverance, and growth. While talent is crucial, understanding the pathways, building relationships, and embracing rejection as part of the process are equally important. This chapter dives deep into actionable steps, industry insights, and real-world tools to help you take your first—or next—big step toward becoming a professional screenwriter.

1. Understanding the Industry Landscape
Screenwriting opportunities exist across a range of platforms, from traditional Hollywood studios to emerging digital platforms. The industry is dynamic, and your approach should be adaptable.

Avenues for Screenwriters:
- Traditional Studios and Production Companies: Warner Bros., Sony Pictures, and Paramount often work with agency-represented writers or those who have proven themselves through contests or smaller projects.
- Streaming Giants: Netflix, Amazon Prime Video, and Hulu are open to unique and diverse voices, producing content across genres.
- Independent Film Markets: Indie films allow new writers to showcase unique perspectives and often serve as a gateway to larger projects.

Emerging Avenues:
- Web Series and Short Films: Platforms like YouTube and Vimeo provide a space to showcase your work to a global audience.
- Interactive Media and Games: Companies like Telltale Games and Quantic Dream are blending screenwriting with interactive storytelling.

Pro Tip: Begin by researching platforms that align with your story's tone and genre to target pitches effectively.

2. Building a Marketable Portfolio
Your portfolio is the first impression you make on potential collaborators. It should reflect your range, voice, and mastery of storytelling.

Essential Elements of a Portfolio:
- A Stellar Spec Script:
  - Write a script in the tone of an existing franchise or show.
  - Example: A spec episode of Succession demonstrates your ability to write complex characters and sharp dialogue.
- Original Content:
  - Include an original screenplay or pilot that showcases your unique voice.
  - Example: Jordan Peele's Get Out balanced a high-concept horror idea with personal and cultural themes.
- Short Films and Web Content:
  - Create or collaborate on short projects to gain practical experience and showcase your work visually.

AI Application: Use AI tools to refine pacing, tone, and character arcs in your scripts before submitting them.

3. Pitching Your Script
A strong pitch is your passport to getting noticed. Whether you're pitching in person, via Zoom, or in a written query, preparation is everything.

A. The Anatomy of a Pitch
- Start with a Hook:
- Your logline should immediately grab attention.
  - Example: "A single mother discovers her child's imaginary friend is a ghost with unfinished business."
- Highlight Core Elements:
- Introduce your protagonist, central conflict, and stakes in 2–3 sentences.
  - Example: "In a world where memories can be extracted and sold, a memory thief uncovers a conspiracy involving his past."
- Communicate Your Vision:
- Share why your story matters and how it connects with contemporary audiences.
  - Example: "This script explores the dangers of unchecked technology while delivering a heart-pounding thriller."

B. Delivering Your Pitch
- Practice Makes Perfect: Rehearse your pitch with friends or mentors.
- Keep It Concise: Aim for a pitch that lasts no more than 90 seconds.
- Be Ready for Questions: Prepare answers about themes, characters, and potential audience.

C. Adapting to Virtual Pitching
With many meetings happening online, perfect your virtual pitch:
- Ensure strong lighting, a quiet environment, and a reliable internet connection.
- Maintain eye contact with the camera to convey confidence.

D. AI as Your Pitch Coach
AI tools can analyze your pitch for clarity and engagement, providing feedback on tone, pacing, and appeal.

Encouragement for Rejections:
Rejections are not the end—they are stepping stones. Even iconic scripts like Pulp Fiction and Deadpool faced years of rejection before finding the right champions. Use rejection as an opportunity to refine your pitch and identify new angles.

4. Networking and Online Resources
Building connections is a critical step toward breaking in. Many forums, websites, and communities can help you find collaborators, mentors, and opportunities.

Websites and Forums to Explore:
- The Black List (blcklst.com):
- A platform for uploading scripts to gain visibility among producers and agents.
- Coverfly (coverfly.com):
- Connects writers with contests, fellowships, and career development opportunities.
- Stage 32 (stage32.com):
- A networking site for screenwriters, filmmakers, and industry professionals.
- Reddit's Screenwriting Subreddit (reddit.com/r/Screenwriting):
- A community where writers share advice, feedback, and industry insights.
- Final Draft Blog (blog.finaldraft.com):
- Offers tips, interviews, and news relevant to screenwriters.

Pro Tip: Regularly engage with these platforms to stay informed about trends, pitch opportunities, and open calls for writers.

5. Real-World Case Studies

Jordan Peele: Get Out
- Journey: Peele's high-concept horror script, blending social commentary with psychological thrills, was initially met with skepticism. After finding the right producer in Blumhouse, Get Out became a cultural phenomenon and won an Oscar for Best Original Screenplay.
- Lesson: Unique stories find their audience when you stay true to your vision.

Diablo Cody: Juno
- Journey: Cody's quirky script caught attention for its witty, authentic dialogue. After entering the right networks, it became a breakout indie success, earning her an Oscar.
- Lesson: Authenticity and a distinct voice can make your work stand out.

Matt Damon and Ben Affleck: Good Will Hunting
- Journey: The duo wrote their script while waiting for acting roles, shopping it to multiple studios before securing a deal. The script launched their careers and won an Oscar.
- Lesson: Perseverance pays off, and writing partnerships can open doors.

Phoebe Waller-Bridge: Fleabag
- Journey: Waller-Bridge adapted her one-woman stage play into a TV script. By blending humor with raw emotion, she created a global hit.
- Lesson: Explore alternative mediums to develop and showcase your ideas.

6. Encouragement and Perspective

Every successful writer has faced rejection. It's part of the journey. For every "yes," there are dozens of "no's." Use rejections as learning opportunities to refine your craft and pitch.

Key Encouragements:
- Rejection is a badge of effort—proof you're putting yourself out there.
- Keep creating. Each new project builds your skill and increases your chances of success.
- Your unique voice is your greatest asset—don't dilute it to fit trends.

7. Practical Exercises
- Pitch Refinement: Write and rehearse a one-minute pitch for your script. Use feedback from peers or AI tools to improve clarity and impact.
- Query Letter Workshop: Write a one-page query letter for your script. Post it in screenwriting forums or use AI tools to analyze its professionalism.
- Industry Research: Choose three production companies or platforms. Research their recent projects and tailor a pitch for one of your scripts.

Conclusion: Breaking In Takes Time
Breaking into the screenwriting industry is a marathon, not a sprint. By building a strong portfolio, mastering the art of pitching, networking effectively, and embracing rejection as part of the process, you can position yourself for success. Use the tools, communities, and resources at your disposal to continue growing as a writer and turning opportunities into realities.

Remember: every great screenwriter started where you are now—with a dream and a blank page.

Chapter 18: Pitching Your Script in the Digital Age

Pitching is an art form, and in today's digital world, it's more dynamic than ever. Whether you're meeting in person, presenting virtually, or submitting written pitches, your ability to convey your story effectively is crucial to success. This chapter delves into the strategies, tools, and techniques needed to craft and deliver compelling pitches, while embracing the opportunities provided by AI and digital platforms.

1. The Fundamentals of a Great Pitch
A successful pitch is concise, engaging, and memorable. It must capture the essence of your story while leaving your audience eager to learn more.

A. Essential Components
  1. The Hook: A one-sentence logline that captures the core of your story.
     ○ Example: "A brilliant janitor at MIT solves impossible math problems while battling his own demons (Good Will Hunting)."
  2. The Core Elements: Briefly describe your protagonist, the central conflict, and the stakes.
     ○ Example: "A divorced father journeys through space to find his lost daughter, only to discover she's leading a rebellion against humanity's colonization efforts."
  3. The Vision: Explain why your story is unique and marketable.
     ○ Example: "This film combines the emotional depth of Arrival with the high-stakes action of Interstellar, exploring themes of family, loyalty, and survival."

B. Clarity and Brevity
Keep your pitch between 60–90 seconds. Focus on the heart of the story without overloading your audience with details.

2. Adapting Your Pitch for Different Formats
A. In-Person Pitching
- Establish a personal connection with your audience.
- Use natural body language and maintain eye contact to convey confidence and passion.
- Have a polished "elevator pitch" ready for impromptu opportunities.

B. Virtual Pitching
- Prepare for technical considerations: ensure good lighting, a reliable internet connection, and a professional background.
- Practice engaging with the camera to simulate direct eye contact.

C. Written Pitches
- Use clear, professional language in query letters or one-page pitch documents.
- Focus on your logline and vision, and personalize your pitch to the recipient.
  - Example Query Opener: "As a lifelong fan of high-stakes thrillers like The Fugitive, I've written a fast-paced script that I believe aligns with your company's recent slate of films."

3. Using AI to Refine and Test Your Pitch
AI can help you polish your pitch and prepare for delivery in the following ways:

A. Feedback and Refinement
- Use AI tools to analyze the tone, clarity, and emotional impact of your logline or pitch.

B. Simulated Audiences
- Test your pitch on AI models that simulate audience responses, identifying areas that might confuse or disengage listeners.

C. Iterative Improvement
- Generate multiple variations of your pitch using AI suggestions, comparing which version resonates best.

4. Building Confidence and Overcoming Rejection
A. Practice Builds Confidence
The more you practice your pitch, the more comfortable and confident you'll become. Record yourself delivering your pitch and review it for tone, pacing, and body language.

B. Rejection Is a Stepping Stone
Every writer faces rejection, often more than once.
- Example: The Shawshank Redemption script was initially dismissed before finding its champion in Castle Rock Entertainment.
- Use rejections as opportunities to refine your pitch or explore new avenues for your work.

C. Staying Positive
Each pitch is a chance to improve. Remember, success in screenwriting often comes after persistence, not perfection.

5. Practical Exercises
- Craft Your Elevator Pitch:
  - Write a 30-second version of your script pitch. Focus on the logline and stakes. Use AI to test for clarity and engagement.
- Simulate a Pitch Meeting:
  - Practice delivering your pitch in front of friends or a camera. Use AI tools to analyze your tone and pacing for improvements.
- Create a One-Page Pitch Document:
  - Summarize your script, including a logline, a paragraph on core elements, and a brief vision statement. Test its effectiveness by sharing it with peers.

6. Real-World Examples of Great Pitches
A. James Cameron and Aliens
Cameron famously pitched Aliens with just two words and a dollar sign: "Alien$." This succinct pitch conveyed the sequel's concept—a bigger, more action-packed continuation of the franchise.

B. Matt Damon and Ben Affleck with Good Will Hunting
The duo pitched their script by emphasizing its mix of humor, drama, and intellectual depth, resonating with producers who saw its crossover potential.

C. Dan Harmon and Rick and Morty
Harmon pitched the show as "a darker, funnier Back to the Future," instantly painting a picture of its tone and premise.

7. Tips for Sustained Success
A. Tailor Each Pitch
No two pitches should be the same. Research the preferences of the person or company you're pitching to and adjust accordingly.

B. Leverage Your Network
Referrals and introductions often increase the likelihood of your pitch being heard. Engage with screenwriting communities, festivals, and forums to expand your network.

C. Keep Innovating
Even if one pitch doesn't land, keep creating. Every new script or idea strengthens your portfolio and increases your chances of success.

8. Encouragement for Aspiring Screenwriters
Rejection is not the end—it's part of the process. Even legendary scripts faced hurdles before finding success.
- Example: Quentin Tarantino's True Romance was rejected by multiple studios before becoming a cult classic.

Use each rejection as an opportunity to grow. Your perseverance, coupled with preparation and passion, will ultimately lead to success.

Conclusion: Mastering the Art of Pitching
Pitching is an essential skill for screenwriters. By crafting a concise, engaging pitch, leveraging AI tools for refinement, and embracing feedback and rejection as steps on your journey, you can confidently present your stories to the industry.

Remember, your voice matters. Every pitch is a chance to share your unique vision with the world.

Chapter 19: Legal and Ethical Considerations in AI Screenwriting

The integration of AI into screenwriting is transforming the creative process, offering tools for idea generation, dialogue refinement, and narrative analysis. However, this innovation comes with legal and ethical responsibilities. Understanding issues like copyright, ownership, and the implications of AI-generated content is essential for writers looking to leverage these tools responsibly. This chapter explores the key legal and ethical considerations in AI screenwriting, offering guidance on protecting your work, respecting intellectual property, and navigating the evolving landscape of AI-assisted creativity.

1. Copyright and Ownership in AI-Assisted Work
A. Who Owns AI-Generated Content?
Ownership of AI-generated work can vary depending on the platform or tool used. Some tools may claim partial rights over the content created with their software.
- Example: A script generated partially by an AI tool like ChatGPT may raise questions about authorship and intellectual property.

How to Protect Yourself:
- Review the terms and conditions of any AI tool before using it.
- Ensure your contributions to the script are substantial and documented to establish your authorship.

B. Copyright Protection for AI-Generated Scripts
Under current laws in many jurisdictions, copyright protection is granted only to works created by humans. This means scripts entirely generated by AI might not qualify for protection.
- Pro Tip: To secure copyright, ensure your human input is clear and significant throughout the writing process.

2. Ethical Use of AI in Screenwriting
A. Avoiding Plagiarism
AI tools trained on vast datasets may inadvertently generate content similar to existing works.
- Best Practice: Always run your scripts through plagiarism-checking tools to ensure originality.

B. Respecting Creative Integrity
AI tools should assist creativity, not replace it. Over-reliance on AI risks producing generic, formulaic scripts that lack personal voice and originality.
- Pro Tip: Use AI for brainstorming and refinement, but let your creativity drive the process.

C. Fair Representation
AI-generated content should reflect diversity and avoid perpetuating harmful stereotypes.
- Example: When using AI to generate character dialogue or settings, review the output for biases or inaccuracies.

3. Licensing AI Tools for Professional Use
When using AI in a professional capacity, ensure you understand the licensing terms of the tools you use.

Common Licensing Models:
- Free Tools: Often have limited functionality and may include restrictions on commercial use.
- Subscription-Based Tools: Offer full features but may retain partial rights to content created using their platforms.
- Enterprise Solutions: Designed for studios and large-scale projects, often with negotiable licensing terms.

Questions to Ask Before Using an AI Tool:
- Does the tool allow for commercial use of generated content?
- Are there limitations on modifying or distributing the content?
- Who owns the output—me or the platform?

4. Navigating Collaborative AI Projects

As AI becomes more integrated into collaborative workflows, writers must establish clear guidelines for credit and ownership.

A. Credit Allocation
- If AI contributes to dialogue refinement or narrative structuring, how should it be credited?
- Best Practice: Clearly differentiate between human and AI contributions in collaborative agreements.

B. Legal Contracts
Include clauses in contracts that specify how AI tools will be used and who retains rights over the final product.

5. Potential Legal Disputes and How to Avoid Them

A. Copyright Infringement
If an AI-generated idea closely resembles an existing work, it could lead to copyright disputes.
- How to Avoid: Use AI as a supplementary tool, not a sole creator, and thoroughly vet your scripts for originality.

B. Data Privacy
Some AI tools require uploading your scripts or ideas, raising concerns about data privacy and misuse.
- How to Protect Yourself: Use reputable platforms with clear data security policies and consider encrypting sensitive information before uploading.

6. The Future of AI and Screenwriting Law

As AI becomes more prominent, laws surrounding AI-generated content are expected to evolve. Writers should stay informed about these changes to protect their rights and navigate the industry responsibly.

Key Areas to Watch:
- Evolving Copyright Laws: Countries like the US and EU are exploring how to classify AI-assisted creations.
- Ethical Standards: Industry organizations may establish guidelines for AI use in creative fields.
- Litigation Precedents: Court cases involving AI-generated works will shape future legal interpretations.

7. Practical Exercises
- Review Terms and Conditions:
  - Choose an AI tool and review its terms of use. Summarize who owns the content and any restrictions on its use.
- Simulate a Collaboration Agreement:
  - Draft a simple contract specifying how AI contributions will be credited and who owns the final script.
- Analyze an AI-Generated Scene:
  - Use an AI tool to generate a short scene, then rewrite it significantly to ensure originality. Compare the two to identify where your creative input added value.

Real-World Case Studies
Case Study 1: AI in Previsualization
A major studio used AI to generate early drafts of dialogue for a sci-fi film. While the tool accelerated the process, the final script underwent substantial human revision to refine character voices and ensure originality.
- Lesson: AI can speed up workflows but shouldn't replace the human touch.

Case Study 2: Ownership Dispute in AI Art
An artist used an AI tool to create illustrations for a project. When the work gained popularity, the AI platform claimed partial ownership based on its terms of use. The dispute highlighted the importance of understanding licensing agreements.
- Lesson: Always clarify ownership rights before using AI tools professionally.

Conclusion: Using AI Responsibly

AI offers incredible opportunities for screenwriters but comes with legal and ethical responsibilities. By staying informed, protecting your rights, and using AI as a tool—not a replacement—you can navigate this evolving landscape with confidence and creativity.

Remember, the heart of screenwriting lies in human storytelling. AI can assist, but your voice is what will ultimately make your work stand out.

Chapter 20: Real-World AI Success Stories in Screenwriting

AI is no longer just a futuristic concept—it's a practical tool reshaping the screenwriting process and the broader film industry. From assisting in script refinement to generating entire story concepts, AI is enabling writers and creators to work more efficiently and innovate in storytelling.

In this chapter, we'll explore real-world examples of AI's impact on screenwriting and filmmaking, highlight the lessons learned from these successes, and provide actionable insights to help you leverage AI in your own creative process.

1. AI in Screenwriting: Success Stories
A. Sunspring: An AI-Generated Short Film
- What Happened: In 2016, filmmaker Oscar Sharp and technologist Ross Goodwin created Sunspring, a short film written entirely by AI. The tool, trained on hundreds of sci-fi screenplays, generated a surreal and enigmatic script.
- Why It's Important: Sunspring showcased the potential of AI for generating unconventional ideas and inspiring creative interpretations.
- Lesson for Writers: While the script was far from polished, it demonstrated AI's capacity to spark ideas that human writers can refine and contextualize.

B. Netflix's Content Recommendations
- What Happened: Netflix uses AI not only to recommend content but also to analyze audience preferences and guide script decisions. For example, AI insights influenced the development of House of Cards by identifying high-demand actors, genres, and themes.
- Why It's Important: This marked a shift toward data-driven storytelling, balancing artistic intuition with audience analysis.
- Lesson for Writers: AI can help you understand market trends and refine your scripts to align with audience expectations without compromising your vision.

C. The Scriptwriter AI Experiment
- What Happened: In collaboration with IBM Watson, a production team used AI to assist in creating a short sci-fi film. Watson analyzed audience preferences, suggested thematic elements, and provided feedback on narrative structure.
- Why It's Important: The project demonstrated how AI can enhance the scriptwriting process by offering insights into audience engagement and improving narrative coherence.
- Lesson for Writers: AI can act as a collaborative partner, guiding your story without dictating its direction.

2. AI in Film Production and Previsualization
A. Avengers: Endgame and Predictive Audience Analysis
- What Happened: Marvel Studios used AI to predict audience reactions to key plot points, helping refine the film's emotional beats.
- Why It's Important: By simulating audience responses, AI ensured that pivotal scenes resonated with viewers.
- Lesson for Writers: Use AI tools to test emotional arcs and optimize critical moments in your screenplay.

B. Previsualization in The Mandalorian
- What Happened: AI-powered tools were used to create virtual sets and previsualizations, enabling directors to experiment with visual storytelling before production.
- Why It's Important: This streamlined the creative process and allowed for greater flexibility in scene composition.
- Lesson for Writers: While previsualization is typically a director's tool, screenwriters can use AI-generated visuals to better communicate their vision in pitch meetings.

3. Lessons From AI-Driven Writing Success
A. Embrace Collaboration
AI works best as a collaborator, enhancing creativity rather than replacing it.
- Example: Writers using AI tools to brainstorm alternative endings or refine dialogue find it sparks fresh ideas while maintaining their creative voice.

B. Balance Data with Creativity
Data-driven storytelling can inform your work but should never overshadow your artistic instincts.
- Example: Netflix's reliance on data for House of Cards didn't dictate the story—it simply ensured its alignment with audience interests.

C. Iterate Quickly
AI accelerates the iterative process, allowing writers to test multiple versions of a scene or dialogue quickly.
- Example: A writer using AI to generate variations of a dramatic monologue can identify the strongest option in minutes.

4. Practical Applications of AI for Writers
A. Refining Emotional Beats
- Use AI to analyze the pacing and tone of your screenplay, ensuring emotional beats land effectively.

B. Generating Ideas
- Input thematic concepts or character descriptions into AI tools to generate alternative plotlines or scene ideas.

C. Audience Simulation
- Simulate audience responses to key plot twists or endings, refining your script based on AI feedback.

5. Exercises for Applying AI Success Lessons
- Brainstorm with AI:
  - Use an AI tool to generate three alternative endings for a scene in your script. Select and refine the strongest option.
- Simulate Audience Feedback:
  - Input your screenplay's logline and a key emotional scene into an AI audience analysis tool. Review the feedback and make adjustments based on engagement levels.
- Analyze a Famous Scene:
  - Choose an iconic scene from a favorite film. Rewrite it with AI assistance to explore how different tones or outcomes might affect the narrative.

6. The Future of AI in Screenwriting
A. Advanced Narrative Tools
AI tools are becoming more sophisticated, offering deeper insights into story structure, character arcs, and audience engagement.

B. Expanding Creative Boundaries
As AI evolves, it will continue to challenge traditional notions of authorship, encouraging writers to experiment and innovate.

C. Ethical and Collaborative Use
AI is a tool, not a replacement. Writers who embrace it responsibly will find new ways to enhance their craft and expand their storytelling possibilities.

Conclusion: Learning From AI Success Stories
AI is transforming screenwriting and filmmaking, offering tools to enhance creativity, streamline workflows, and understand audiences better. By learning from real-world examples and leveraging these tools responsibly, you can unlock new dimensions in your writing and storytelling.

Remember, the future of screenwriting isn't about machines replacing humans—it's about empowering writers with tools that amplify their creativity.

Chapter 21: How to Self-Publish and Market Your Screenplay

In today's digital age, writers have more control than ever over their creative work. Self-publishing your screenplay allows you to bypass traditional gatekeepers, showcase your talent, and attract potential collaborators, producers, and fans. However, success requires more than just uploading your work—you need a strategy to market it effectively.

This chapter explores how to self-publish your screenplay, build an audience, and leverage digital tools to gain visibility.

1. Why Self-Publish Your Screenplay?
A. Creative Control
Self-publishing allows you to present your screenplay exactly as you envision it, without compromising on creative choices.

B. Direct Audience Access
By self-publishing, you can connect directly with readers, filmmakers, and industry professionals, creating opportunities for collaboration and feedback.

C. Portfolio Building
A self-published screenplay can showcase your talent and expand your portfolio, making you more attractive to potential agents, producers, or collaborators.

2. Preparing Your Screenplay for Self-Publishing
Before publishing, ensure your screenplay is polished and professionally formatted.

A. Formatting Standards
Follow industry-standard formatting to make your screenplay readable and professional.
- Recommended Tools:
    - Final Draft (finaldraft.com)
    - Celtx (celtx.com)
    - WriterDuet (writerduet.com)

B. Editing and Proofreading
Collaborate with a professional editor or trusted peers to refine your script.
- Use AI tools like Grammarly or ProWritingAid to catch typos and improve clarity.

C. Writing an Engaging Synopsis
Your synopsis should be concise and captivating, summarizing your story's core elements while leaving readers wanting more.
- Example: "In a dystopian future, a rebellious scientist uncovers a government conspiracy that threatens humanity's survival."

3. Choosing a Platform for Self-Publishing

Several platforms cater to screenwriters looking to self-publish and distribute their work. These platforms provide opportunities to share your screenplay with a wider audience, connect with industry professionals, and even monetize your work.

A. Platforms for Screenplay Publishing:
Amazon Kindle Direct Publishing (KDP):
Publish your screenplay as an eBook or print-on-demand paperback, reaching readers worldwide.
Website: kdp.amazon.com

The Black List:
Upload your screenplay to gain visibility among producers, agents, and industry professionals.
Website: blcklst.com

Stage 32:
Share your screenplay with a community of filmmakers, producers, and screenwriters, and participate in networking opportunities.
Website: stage32.com

Google Play Books Partner Center:
Publish your screenplay as an eBook on the Google Play Store to reach a global audience.
Website: play.google.com/books/publish

Script Revolution:
A free platform for showcasing your screenplay to filmmakers and producers, with options for marketing and visibility.
Website: scriptrevolution.com

BBC Writersroom:
Submit your screenplay during specific submission windows for a chance to collaborate with the BBC.
Website: bbc.co.uk/writersroom

International Screenwriters' Association (ISA):
Showcase your screenplay, access writing opportunities, and connect with industry professionals.
Website: networkisa.org

Open Screenplay:
Collaborate, create, and showcase screenplays on this platform, with opportunities for contests and industry recognition.
Website: openscreenplay.com

Wattpad:
Share your screenplay and stories with a large, engaged audience, potentially leading to publishing or adaptation opportunities.
Website: wattpad.com

A Word of Caution: Protect Your Screenplay
Before uploading your screenplay to any platform, take steps to protect your intellectual property:

- Register Your Screenplay: Use an official copyright office (e.g., the U.S. Copyright Office) or a recognized organization like the Writers Guild of America (WGA) to secure your rights.
- Keep Records: Save drafts, emails, and other materials that document your ownership of the work.
- Understand Platform Terms: Review the platform's terms and conditions to ensure you retain control over your screenplay.

Taking these precautions ensures that your work remains protected while you leverage these platforms to share your vision with the world.

4. Marketing Your Screenplay
A. Building Your Brand
Establishing a personal brand helps you stand out in the crowded creative space.

- Create a Professional Website: Showcase your screenplays, bio, and contact information.
  - Website Builder Tools: Squarespace, Wix, or WordPress.
- Leverage Social Media: Use platforms like Twitter, Instagram, and LinkedIn to share insights, engage with followers, and promote your work.

B. Leveraging Online Communities
- Participate in forums and groups like Reddit's r/Screenwriting or Facebook's screenwriting communities to share your screenplay and gather feedback.
- Engage on platforms like Coverfly to connect with contests and development labs.

C. Hosting Virtual Events
- Organize online table reads with actors to bring your screenplay to life and generate buzz.
- Host webinars or Q&A sessions about your writing process.

D. Networking at Film Festivals
Even as a self-published writer, attending festivals like Sundance or SXSW can help you meet industry professionals and promote your work.

5. Monetizing Your Screenplay
Self-publishing doesn't just showcase your work—it can generate income if marketed effectively.

A. Selling Your Screenplay
- Set a fair price for your screenplay on platforms like Amazon or Gumroad.

B. Licensing Opportunities
- Market your screenplay for licensing deals with production companies or independent filmmakers.

C. Merchandise and Add-Ons
- Create supplementary content like "behind-the-scenes" eBooks, character backstories, or annotated script versions for fans.

6. Using AI to Optimize Your Efforts
A. Refining Your Marketing Copy
AI tools like Copy.ai or Jasper can help craft compelling blurbs, social media posts, and email pitches.

B. Audience Analysis
Use AI-driven tools to analyze your screenplay's potential audience demographics and preferences.
- Example: Google Analytics or AI-based market research platforms can help target your ideal audience.

C. Generating Visual Content
Create promotional visuals for your screenplay using AI design tools like Canva or Adobe Firefly.

7. Real-World Examples of Successful Self-Publishing

A. Andy Weir's The Martian
- What Happened: Weir initially self-published The Martian as a serialized story on his blog, then as an eBook on Amazon. Its success led to a major publishing deal and a blockbuster film adaptation.
- Lesson: Building a loyal audience through self-publishing can lead to significant opportunities.

B. E.L. James and Fifty Shades of Grey
- What Happened: James self-published her novel, which became a cultural phenomenon and inspired a film trilogy.
- Lesson: Effective self-promotion and word-of-mouth can transform self-published works into mainstream hits.

C. Ava DuVernay's Early Screenwriting Career
- What Happened: DuVernay leveraged indie and self-funded projects to establish herself as a director and screenwriter, eventually leading to larger studio opportunities.
- Lesson: Small, independent projects can showcase your talent and open doors to bigger opportunities.

8. Practical Exercises
- Publish a Short Screenplay:
  - Choose a short screenplay and self-publish it on a platform like Script Revolution. Use the experience to learn the publishing process.
- Create a Marketing Plan:
  - Write a 30-day promotional plan for your screenplay, including social media posts, email campaigns, and community engagement.
- Host a Table Read:
  - Organize a virtual or in-person table read of your screenplay. Record the session and use it as a promotional tool.

Conclusion: Taking Control of Your Creative Journey
Self-publishing and marketing your screenplay empowers you to take control of your creative career. By leveraging digital platforms, building your audience, and using AI to refine your efforts, you can showcase your talent, gain visibility, and create new opportunities in the industry.

Remember, success in self-publishing is a marathon, not a sprint. Each step you take—publishing, promoting, and engaging with your audience—brings you closer to achieving your screenwriting goals.

Chapter 22: Overcoming Writer's Block with AI

Writer's block is a common challenge for screenwriters, but it doesn't have to stop you in your tracks. With AI as a creative partner, you can generate new ideas, overcome obstacles, and keep your creative momentum alive. This chapter explores how to use AI tools to brainstorm, experiment, and rediscover inspiration when you're stuck.

1. Understanding Writer's Block
Writer's block can manifest in different ways:
- Blank Page Syndrome: Struggling to start a scene or script.
- Mid-Story Stagnation: Losing momentum or direction halfway through.
- Idea Overload: Having too many concepts to focus on one.

Each type of writer's block requires a tailored solution, and AI offers tools to address them all.

2. Using AI to Generate New Ideas
AI tools can help spark creativity by offering fresh perspectives and breaking through mental blocks.
A. Brainstorming Scene Concepts
- Example Tool: ChatGPT or Sudowrite
   o Input: "A romantic comedy scene in a crowded train station."
   o Output: Ideas for meet-cute moments, conflicts, and dialogue.

B. Expanding Story Premises
- How to Use AI: Provide a logline or story idea, and ask AI to expand it into a detailed outline.
   o Input: "A lonely AI robot befriends a human child in a post-apocalyptic world."
   o Output: Scene ideas, character arcs, and possible endings.

C. Generating "What-If" Scenarios
- Exercise: Use AI to explore "What if" questions for your story.
   o Example: "What if the antagonist was secretly helping the protagonist?"

3. Breaking Through Mid-Story Stagnation
When you lose direction in the middle of a script, AI can help refocus and reinvigorate your writing.
A. Scene Continuations
- Example Tool: Jasper or Writesonic
  - Input the last line of a scene and ask AI to suggest the next action or dialogue.
  - Example: "The detective finds a bloodstained note but doesn't know what it means."   AI suggests the note's contents and potential suspects.

B. Character Development Prompts
- Ask AI questions about your characters to uncover hidden motivations or backstory details.
  - Example: "What secret is my protagonist hiding from the audience?"

4. Experimenting with Structure and Style
AI tools can inspire new approaches to narrative structure or writing style.
A. Exploring Nonlinear Structures
- Use AI to suggest alternative scene orders or experiment with nonlinear storytelling.
  - Example: "What if the story starts with the ending and unfolds in reverse?"

B. Adapting Style to Genre
- Input a scene and ask AI to rewrite it in a specific genre or tone.
  - Example: Rewrite a romantic scene as a suspenseful thriller.

5. Exercises for Overcoming Writer's Block with AI
Exercise 1: Dialogue Starter
- Input a character description and ask AI to generate dialogue for a specific situation.
  - Example: "A sarcastic teenager arguing with their strict parent about curfew."

Exercise 2: Plot Twist Generator
- Provide your story's premise and ask AI for three possible plot twists.
  - Example: "In a heist film, what unexpected obstacle could derail the plan?"

Exercise 3: Writing Warm-Up
- Use AI to generate a random prompt and write a quick scene based on it.
  - Example Prompt: "A stranded astronaut discovers a strange message on the moon."

6. Real-World Examples of AI-Assisted Creativity
Example 1: Collaborative Writing with AI
A screenwriter struggling with Act II used Sudowrite to brainstorm subplots. The tool suggested a new character dynamic that enriched the story and resolved pacing issues.

Example 2: Revitalizing a Script's Tone
A filmmaker used AI to rewrite scenes with a more comedic tone, transforming a struggling drama into a dark comedy that won accolades at festivals.

7. Encouragement and Perspective
Writer's block is a temporary hurdle, not a permanent barrier. AI tools provide a collaborative space to experiment, make mistakes, and find solutions without judgment. Remember, every writer faces challenges—what matters is how you overcome them.

Conclusion: Writing Without Limits
With AI as your ally, writer's block becomes an opportunity for growth and discovery. By embracing these tools, you can break through creative walls, reignite your passion for storytelling, and transform roadblocks into stepping stones.

Remember, the creative spark always begins with you—AI is here to amplify, not replace, your vision.

Chapter 23: The AI-Assisted Revision Process

Revising a screenplay is where good stories become great. It's a process of tightening dialogue, refining character arcs, strengthening structure, and ensuring the emotional beats resonate with your audience. AI tools can streamline and enhance this process, acting as a virtual "script doctor" to help polish your work with precision.

This chapter explores how to use AI for script revision, offering step-by-step strategies and practical examples.

1. The Importance of Revisions
Revising isn't just about fixing mistakes—it's about elevating your screenplay to its fullest potential. Key areas to focus on during revisions include:
- Dialogue: Does it sound natural and authentic?
- Structure: Are the plot points clear and impactful?
- Pacing: Does the story maintain engagement throughout?
- Character Arcs: Do characters grow in meaningful ways?

2. Leveraging AI Tools for Revisions
A. Analyzing Dialogue for Clarity and Impact
AI tools can evaluate dialogue for tone, subtext, and authenticity.
- Example Tool: ChatGPT or Sudowrite
    o Input: A snippet of dialogue.
    o Output: Suggestions for improving tone, making dialogue more concise, or adding subtext.
    o Example: "Your protagonist's dialogue sounds formal. Consider a more conversational tone to match their personality."

B. Strengthening Story Structure
AI can identify plot inconsistencies and suggest ways to streamline your narrative.
- Example Tool: Plottr or Dramatica Pro
    o Use AI to map your story beats against common structures (e.g., three-act or hero's journey).

C. Pacing Analysis
AI can flag scenes that drag or feel rushed.
- Example Tool: Final Draft's AI-Powered Insights
    o Output: "Scenes 5–7 feel slow compared to the action-packed opening. Consider trimming redundant dialogue."

D. Checking Emotional Beats
AI can help ensure your screenplay hits the intended emotional notes.
- Example Tool: Grammarly for Tone Analysis or Hemingway App
  - Feedback: "The climax lacks emotional intensity. Consider adding a character revelation or higher stakes."

3. Practical Steps for AI-Assisted Revisions
Step 1: Identify Problem Areas
- Run your script through an AI tool to highlight common issues like:
  - Overused words or phrases.
  - Inconsistent character voice.
  - Redundant or repetitive scenes.

Step 2: Experiment with Alternatives
- Use AI to generate multiple versions of a scene or dialogue. Compare them to find the best fit.
  - Example: "Rewrite this scene with more tension between the protagonist and antagonist."

Step 3: Test for Consistency
- AI tools can analyze whether characters act and speak consistently throughout the script.
  - Example: "Does this character's voice stay sarcastic and witty, as established in earlier scenes?"

4. Exercises for Revising Your Script with AI
- Dialogue Refinement Exercise:
  - Choose a pivotal dialogue scene. Input it into an AI tool for feedback on tone and subtext. Rewrite based on suggestions.
- Scene Consolidation Exercise:
  - Select two consecutive scenes and ask AI to suggest ways to combine them without losing key information.
- Tone Adjustment Exercise:
  - Input a scene and request a tone shift (e.g., comedic to dramatic). Compare the revised tone to your original.

5. Real-World Examples of AI in Revisions
Example 1: Fixing Dialogue Consistency
A writer used AI to flag moments where a supporting character's tone shifted inconsistently. The revisions made the character's voice more coherent and engaging.

Example 2: Strengthening a Weak Act II
An AI tool analyzed the pacing of a script's second act and suggested adding a subplot to maintain momentum. The writer implemented the change, which improved the story's flow.

Example 3: Refining a Climax
A screenwriter struggling with an underwhelming climax used AI to brainstorm higher-stakes scenarios, resulting in a more impactful ending.

6. Balancing Human Creativity with AI Assistance
While AI is a powerful tool, it's essential to maintain your creative voice throughout the revision process.

A. Use AI as a Partner, Not a Replacement
AI can highlight problems and offer suggestions, but you should make the final decisions to preserve your story's originality.

B. Trust Your Instincts
If AI's suggestions don't align with your vision, prioritize your instincts. Use AI as a guide, not an authority.

C. Iterate and Refine
Revisions are iterative. Use AI to explore multiple possibilities, then refine the best options further.

7. Encouragement for the Revision Process

Revising a screenplay can feel overwhelming, but it's also an opportunity to discover new layers of creativity. Remember:

- Every draft brings you closer to your best work.
- AI tools are here to support, not replace, your unique vision.
- The revision process is where good stories transform into unforgettable ones.

Conclusion: Your Virtual Script Doctor

The revision process is where your screenplay truly takes shape, and AI tools can be invaluable in helping you refine and polish every element. From dialogue to pacing, structure to tone, AI offers insights and alternatives to elevate your story while leaving the final creative decisions in your hands.

With persistence, curiosity, and the right tools, your screenplay can achieve its full potential.

Chapter 24: Building and Refining a Long-Term Career

Screenwriting is not just about crafting a single script—it's about building a sustainable career. Whether you're seeking representation, managing submissions, or tracking feedback, a strategic approach is essential. With AI tools and modern career-building techniques, you can streamline your efforts, focus on growth, and increase your opportunities in the industry.

This chapter explores how to build a long-term career as a screenwriter, leveraging AI and professional best practices to refine your craft, manage your work, and expand your network.

1. Crafting a Long-Term Vision for Your Career
A. Set Clear Goals
Define what success means to you.
- Examples:
  - Land representation with a top talent agency.
  - Sell an original screenplay.
  - Transition from writing short films to feature-length projects.

B. Create a Career Plan
Break your goals into achievable milestones.
- Short-Term Goals: Write two spec scripts, network at a film festival.
- Long-Term Goals: Secure an agent, option a screenplay, work on a TV series.

Pro Tip: Revisit and adjust your career plan annually to align with your evolving aspirations.

2. Building and Managing Your Portfolio
A. Showcase Versatility
Include a variety of works in your portfolio, such as:
- Original screenplays.
- Spec scripts for existing shows.
- Short films or pilots.

B. Keep Your Portfolio Updated
Regularly revise your scripts based on feedback and industry trends.

C. Use AI to Optimize Your Portfolio
- AI tools like Grammarly or Final Draft can refine formatting and language.
- Platforms like Coverfly or The Black List offer feedback and visibility for your work.

3. Networking and Collaboration
A. Build Relationships in the Industry
Networking is essential for sustained success.
- Attend film festivals, screenwriting conferences, and workshops.
- Join screenwriting communities like Stage 32 or Reddit's r/Screenwriting.

B. Collaborate with Other Creatives
Partnering with directors, producers, or other writers can open doors.
- Use platforms like ScreenCraft or Script Revolution to find collaborators.

4. Tracking Submissions and Feedback
A. Stay Organized
Use a tracking system to manage your submissions.
- Include fields for script titles, submission dates, response statuses, and feedback.

B. Leverage AI for Analysis
- AI tools like Notion or Trello can create automated workflows for tracking submissions.
- AI sentiment analysis tools can help evaluate feedback for actionable insights.

5. Navigating Industry Trends and Changes
A. Adapt to Evolving Formats
Streaming platforms, interactive storytelling, and AI-generated media are reshaping the industry. Stay informed about emerging opportunities.
- Pro Tip: Study successful works on platforms like Netflix or Hulu to identify trends.

B. Diversify Your Skills
- Learn adjacent skills like directing, editing, or game writing to increase your marketability.
- Use AI tools to experiment with formats like VR scripts or interactive narratives.

6. Using AI to Support Long-Term Growth
A. Idea Management
Store and organize your story ideas with AI-powered tools like Evernote or Obsidian, which can tag and categorize concepts for easy retrieval.

B. Skill Development
Use AI to analyze your scripts against successful screenplays, identifying areas for improvement.

C. Personal Branding
- AI tools like Canva or Adobe Firefly can help create professional pitch decks, social media posts, and personal branding materials.

7. Practical Exercises for Career Growth
- Create a Networking Plan:
  - List three industry events you'll attend this year. Research attendees and prepare questions or pitches in advance.
- Update Your Portfolio:
  - Choose one script to polish with AI tools. Ensure it reflects your current skill level and aligns with industry standards.
- Set Annual Goals:
  - Write down three career goals for the next year. Break them into actionable steps and set deadlines for each.

8. Real-World Success Stories
A. Phoebe Waller-Bridge: From Stage to Screen
Waller-Bridge started with a one-woman stage play (Fleabag) before adapting it into an award-winning series.
- Lesson: Diversifying formats and collaborating with the right partners can elevate your career.

B. Taylor Sheridan: Building a Screenwriting Brand
Sheridan wrote gritty, character-driven scripts (Sicario, Hell or High Water) that carved out a niche for him in Hollywood.
- Lesson: Focus on your unique voice to stand out.

C. Ava DuVernay: Leveraging Independent Projects
DuVernay gained recognition by writing and directing indie films before transitioning to studio projects (Selma, A Wrinkle in Time).
- Lesson: Independent projects can serve as stepping stones to larger opportunities.

9. Encouragement for the Long Haul
Building a screenwriting career takes time and persistence. Setbacks are part of the process, but every rejection or stalled project brings you closer to success. Remember:
- Your unique voice and perspective are your greatest assets.
- Progress is cumulative—each script, connection, and lesson adds to your growth.
- Stay adaptable, curious, and committed to your craft.

Conclusion: Your Career, Your Journey
A successful screenwriting career isn't built overnight. With a clear vision, consistent effort, and the support of AI tools, you can refine your craft, expand your network, and achieve your goals. Embrace the journey, trust your voice, and keep writing—the best stories are still ahead.

Chapter 25: Exploring AI-Enhanced Tools for Writers

The evolution of artificial intelligence has introduced screenwriters to a new era of creative tools. From idea generation to script analysis, AI-powered platforms can streamline your process, inspire new concepts, and refine your storytelling.

This chapter explores the best AI tools available, their practical applications, and how to integrate them into your writing workflow.

1. Categories of AI Tools for Screenwriters
AI tools can be divided into several key categories, each tailored to a specific stage of the writing process.
A. Brainstorming and Idea Generation
- Examples of Tools:
    - ChatGPT (openai.com): Generate story ideas, explore plot twists, or refine loglines.
    - Sudowrite (sudowrite.com): Offers writing prompts and creative suggestions for overcoming writer's block.
- Use Case:
    - Input: "A fantasy world where humans coexist with sentient plants."
    - Output: Ideas for settings, characters, and conflicts.

B. Script Formatting and Organization
- Examples of Tools:
    - Final Draft (finaldraft.com): Industry-standard software for script formatting and storyboarding.
    - WriterDuet (writerduet.com): Cloud-based platform for collaborative scriptwriting.
- Use Case: Automatically format your screenplay to meet industry standards.

C. Narrative and Character Analysis
- Examples of Tools:
    - Dramatica Pro (dramatica.com): Analyzes narrative structure and suggests ways to enhance storytelling.
    - ProWritingAid (prowritingaid.com): Checks for grammar, pacing, and tone issues.
- Use Case: Analyze a character arc to ensure consistency and emotional resonance.

D. Sound and Visual Integration
- Examples of Tools:
  - Suno.AI (suno.ai): Generates soundscapes and musical motifs based on story tone.
  - Runway (runwayml.com): Assists in creating visuals for storyboards and previsualization.
- Use Case: Develop an audio or visual representation of a scene to enhance pitches or guide production.

2. How to Use AI Tools Effectively
A. Enhance, Don't Replace
AI tools are best used as creative collaborators, not replacements for your unique storytelling voice.
- Tip: Use AI to refine existing ideas rather than generate entire scripts from scratch.

B. Experiment and Iterate
Leverage AI to explore alternative scenarios, dialogue options, or narrative structures.
- Example: Ask an AI tool to rewrite a scene with increased tension or comedic undertones, then evaluate the results.

C. Test for Audience Engagement
Some AI tools simulate audience reactions, helping you gauge how your script might resonate.
- Example Tool: Readable or Grammarly's tone analysis.

3. Practical Exercises for Writers
- Idea Expansion Exercise:
  - Use ChatGPT or Sudowrite to brainstorm five alternative directions for a scene in your screenplay. Compare the suggestions and choose one to develop further.
- Dialogue Analysis Exercise:
  - Input a dialogue-heavy scene into ProWritingAid. Review the feedback and rewrite the scene to improve pacing and subtext.
- Sound and Visual Cue Development:
  - Use Suno.AI or Runway to create a soundscape or visual representation for a pivotal scene. Incorporate these elements into your screenplay.

4. Real-World Examples of AI-Enhanced Writing
Example 1: Previsualization in Animation
An independent filmmaker used Runway to create a visual
storyboard for their animated short. This helped secure funding by
clearly conveying the story's vision.

Example 2: Refining a Character Arc
A screenwriter used Dramatica Pro to identify inconsistencies in
their protagonist's emotional journey. The insights helped align the
character's arc with the story's central themes.

Example 3: Sound Design Integration
A writer experimenting with AI-generated soundscapes from
Suno.AI used the tool to build immersive atmospheres for a sci-fi
script, impressing potential collaborators during a pitch meeting.

5. Ethical Considerations When Using AI Tools
A. Originality vs. Over-Reliance
While AI can suggest ideas, ensure your final work reflects your
unique voice.
- Pro Tip: Use plagiarism-checking tools to verify originality
  when working with AI-generated content.

B. Ownership and Licensing
Review the terms and conditions of any AI tool to understand
content ownership and licensing implications.
- Example: Some platforms retain partial rights to AI-generated
  outputs.

6. The Future of AI-Enhanced Writing
As AI evolves, new tools will continue to emerge, offering:
- Deeper Narrative Analysis: AI tools that understand story arcs
  and audience psychology.
- Immersive Development Platforms: Integration of VR and AR
  for script visualization.
- Collaborative AI: Tools that adapt to your unique style and
  preferences over time.

7. Encouragement for Writers Exploring AI

AI is a powerful ally, but your creativity and perspective are irreplaceable. Embrace these tools as opportunities to experiment, refine, and enhance your storytelling. The combination of your vision and AI's capabilities can unlock new dimensions in your craft.

Emerging AI Tools and Future Trends

The field of AI is evolving rapidly, and new tools are emerging that offer even greater possibilities for screenwriters. Here are a few groundbreaking innovations to watch for:

1. AI-Powered Scene Visualizers:
   - Tools like Runway Gen-2 are advancing into real-time video generation, allowing writers to visualize scenes as cinematic sequences.
2. Voice Generation and Soundscapes:
   - Platforms like ElevenLabs enable writers to generate character voices for table reads, bringing dialogue to life.
3. Interactive Story Development Platforms:
   - Tools like Altered AI are experimenting with branching narrative frameworks for interactive storytelling, empowering writers to craft immersive experiences for games or VR.
4. Emotion Analysis and Audience Prediction:
   - Emerging tools are focusing on predictive analytics, simulating audience reactions to emotional beats, character arcs, and plot twists.
5. AI-Driven Collaboration Spaces:
   - Integrated platforms like Notion AI are becoming creative hubs where writers, editors, and collaborators can co-develop scripts in real-time with AI assistance.

Future-Proofing Your Workflow: Staying informed about these tools and integrating them into your creative process will ensure you remain ahead of industry trends, continuously refining and innovating your storytelling techniques.

Conclusion: Empowering Writers with AI Tools

AI tools are transforming the way screenwriters approach storytelling, offering unprecedented opportunities for innovation and efficiency. By integrating these technologies into your workflow, you can push the boundaries of your creativity, streamline the writing process, and elevate your scripts to new heights.

Remember, AI is here to support your journey—not replace your unique storytelling voice.

Chapter 26: Case Studies of Iconic Scripts

Some screenplays stand out as benchmarks of storytelling excellence, capturing audiences and influencing generations of writers. By studying these iconic scripts, we can uncover what makes them effective and apply these lessons to our own writing. AI tools add another dimension to this analysis, offering insights into patterns, pacing, and emotional resonance.

This chapter explores detailed case studies of legendary screenplays and demonstrates how AI-driven analysis can help you replicate their success.

1. Why Study Iconic Scripts?
Great scripts offer timeless lessons on structure, character development, and audience engagement. By dissecting these works, writers can:
- Understand how pacing and structure enhance narrative flow.
- Learn how dialogue and subtext reveal character and conflict.
- Explore techniques for creating emotional resonance and thematic depth.

AI Advantage: AI tools can analyze scripts at scale, identifying patterns and suggesting applications for your own work.

2. Case Study: Inception (2010)
Overview:
Christopher Nolan's Inception is a masterclass in layered storytelling, balancing a complex narrative with emotional depth.

Key Elements:
1. Structure: The nested-dream format is meticulously layered, creating tension and momentum.
2. Character Stakes: Cobb's internal struggle (returning to his children) grounds the high-concept premise.
3. Themes: The film explores themes of reality, guilt, and redemption.

AI Insights:
- Structure Analysis: AI tools can map the dream levels, identifying how each layer escalates tension.
  - Example: The pacing accelerates with shorter sequences as the dreams progress deeper.
- Character Arcs: AI highlights how Cobb's emotional journey anchors the film amidst its intricate plot.

Lesson for Writers: Even the most complex narratives must have a clear emotional throughline to resonate with audiences.

3. Case Study: Parasite (2019)
Overview:
Bong Joon-ho's Parasite blends dark comedy and thriller elements to deliver a biting critique of class inequality.

Key Elements:
- Structure: The story's midpoint twist transforms it from a dark comedy into a tense thriller.
- Subtext: Every interaction is loaded with unspoken class commentary.
- Visual Storytelling: The use of space (upstairs vs. downstairs) reinforces themes of power and privilege.

AI Insights:
- Pacing Analysis: AI tools show how the midpoint twist dramatically shifts the story's tempo, increasing tension.
- Subtext Detection: AI can identify recurring motifs (rain, stairs) and their symbolic connections to class dynamics.

Lesson for Writers: Use subtext and visual metaphors to enhance the emotional and thematic impact of your story.

4. Case Study: The Social Network (2010)
Overview:
Aaron Sorkin's sharp, dialogue-driven script for The Social Network captures the rise of Facebook through the lens of betrayal and ambition.

Key Elements:
- Dialogue: Witty, fast-paced exchanges reveal character dynamics and escalate conflict.
- Structure: The dual timelines (legal depositions and flashbacks) keep the narrative engaging.
- Themes: The film examines power, loyalty, and the cost of success.

AI Insights:
- Dialogue Analysis: AI highlights how Sorkin's dialogue maintains character distinction while driving the plot.
- Emotional Beats: Tools can analyze how key scenes (e.g., Zuckerberg's isolation) align with audience engagement trends.

Lesson for Writers: Dynamic dialogue can carry complex narratives while keeping characters vivid and relatable.

5. Applying These Lessons to Your Writing
A. Use AI to Analyze Your Script
- Run your screenplay through tools like Dramatica Pro or Plottr to identify structural strengths and weaknesses.

B. Focus on Character Arcs
- Ensure that each character has a clear emotional journey. Use AI to test consistency in tone and motivation.

C. Experiment with Subtext
- Input scenes into an AI tool and ask it to suggest layers of meaning or symbolic elements to enhance your story.

6. Exercises for Learning from Case Studies
- Analyze a Scene:
  - Choose a pivotal scene from one of these films and break it down for structure, pacing, and subtext. Rewrite a similar scene in your screenplay.
- AI Structure Comparison:
  - Map your script's structure against one of these films using AI tools. Identify areas where pacing or narrative beats could improve.
- Dialogue Practice:
  - Write a scene inspired by Sorkin's fast-paced dialogue style. Use AI to analyze rhythm and tone for refinement.

7. Encouragement for Writers
Studying iconic scripts is a powerful way to learn the craft of screenwriting. By applying these lessons and leveraging AI tools, you can refine your storytelling, elevate your scripts, and create work that resonates deeply with audiences.

Conclusion: Learn from the Best, Innovate with AI
Iconic scripts like Inception, Parasite, and The Social Network demonstrate the heights screenwriting can achieve. With AI-driven analysis, you can uncover the mechanics of these masterpieces and adapt their techniques to your unique voice.

The next iconic script could be yours—let these lessons inspire you to push the boundaries of your storytelling.

Chapter 27: Writing for a World with AI-Generated Content

As AI-generated content becomes increasingly prevalent in storytelling, screenwriters face new challenges and opportunities. While AI can generate compelling ideas and scripts, it lacks the emotional depth, originality, and nuance that only human creativity can provide. To thrive in this landscape, writers must embrace AI as a tool while honing the unique qualities that make their stories stand out.

This chapter explores the rise of AI-generated content, the implications for screenwriters, and strategies for maintaining creative authenticity in an AI-saturated industry.

1. The Rise of AI-Generated Content
AI-generated stories are gaining traction across various media, including:
- Films: Short films like Sunspring demonstrated AI's ability to generate scripts, though they still require significant human refinement.
- Interactive Media: AI tools are driving dynamic storytelling in games and VR experiences.
- Serialized Content: AI is increasingly being used to analyze trends and inform the creation of binge-worthy TV series.

2. Challenges for Screenwriters
A. Increased Competition
AI tools make it easier for anyone to generate scripts, increasing the volume of content in the market.

B. Perception of Value
Producers and studios may view AI-generated scripts as a faster, cheaper alternative to human writing, raising questions about the perceived value of human creativity.

C. Risk of Generic Content
Over-reliance on AI can lead to formulaic stories that lack the originality and emotional resonance audiences crave.

3. Opportunities for Writers
A. Combining Human Creativity with AI Efficiency
Writers who master AI tools can produce high-quality content
faster without sacrificing their unique voice.

B. Tapping Into Emerging Markets
AI-generated content is creating demand for writers who can refine,
humanize, and elevate these scripts.

C. Standing Out Through Authenticity
Originality, emotional depth, and personal experiences are areas
where human writers will always have an edge over AI.

4. Strategies for Thriving in an AI-Driven Industry
A. Embrace AI as a Collaborative Tool
- Use AI for brainstorming, generating alternatives, and refining
  existing ideas.
- Example: If AI generates a predictable plot twist, think of ways
  to subvert it with your own creative spin.

B. Focus on Emotional Resonance
AI struggles to replicate the complexities of human emotions. Make
your scripts emotionally impactful by:
- Crafting relatable, multi-dimensional characters.
- Exploring universal themes like love, loss, and identity.

C. Cultivate a Distinct Voice
A unique writing style is your greatest asset. To develop your voice:
- Study iconic screenwriters known for their distinct tones (e.g.,
  Aaron Sorkin, Greta Gerwig).
- Practice writing scenes in multiple genres to identify your
  strengths.

D. Stay Informed About Industry Trends
- Follow platforms like The Black List and Coverfly to
  understand what types of stories are gaining traction.
- Use AI tools to analyze market trends and audience
  preferences.

5. Practical Exercises for Writers
- AI Collaboration Exercise:
  - Use an AI tool to generate a short scene. Rewrite it with a focus on adding emotional depth and originality.
- Theme Exploration Exercise:
  - Identify a universal theme (e.g., redemption) and write a scene that conveys it through character actions and dialogue.
- Trend Analysis Exercise:
  - Research a popular TV show or film. Use AI to analyze its themes, pacing, and structure, then write a pitch for a similar but original concept.

6. Ethical Considerations for Writers
A. Maintaining Creative Integrity
AI should assist, not overshadow, your creative process. Always prioritize originality and authenticity.

B. Balancing Innovation with Responsibility
As AI evolves, ensure its use aligns with ethical storytelling practices, avoiding stereotypes and clichés.

C. Protecting Your Work
Understand the terms of use for any AI tools you integrate into your workflow to ensure your content remains protected.

7. Encouragement for Writers
AI may reshape the landscape, but your creativity and unique perspective will always be in demand. Embrace the tools available, adapt to the changes, and continue honing your craft. The future of storytelling needs writers who can innovate while staying true to the human experience.

Conclusion: Embracing the Future of Screenwriting
In a world increasingly influenced by AI-generated content, screenwriters have the opportunity to redefine what it means to tell a great story. By combining the efficiency of AI with the emotional depth and originality of human creativity, you can carve out your place in this evolving industry.

Remember, AI can assist—but it's your voice, imagination, and perspective that will set your work apart.

Chapter 28: Emerging Trends in Storytelling

Storytelling is evolving at an unprecedented pace, driven by technological advancements, shifting audience preferences, and the integration of AI. Screenwriters who stay ahead of these trends can not only remain relevant but also pioneer new formats and genres.

This chapter examines emerging storytelling trends, the role of AI in shaping them, and actionable insights to help writers adapt and innovate.

1. The Rise of Interactive and Immersive Storytelling
A. Branching Narratives
Interactive storytelling formats, such as those in video games and interactive films like Bandersnatch, allow audiences to make choices that affect the story's outcome.
- Opportunities for Writers:
  - Create multiple storylines that branch seamlessly while maintaining narrative coherence.
  - Write emotionally compelling decision points that resonate with diverse audience experiences.

B. Immersive Technologies
Virtual Reality (VR) and Augmented Reality (AR) are enabling fully immersive storytelling experiences.
- Example: Wolves in the Walls (VR) uses AR to place audiences inside a story, interacting with characters and influencing events.
- Pro Tip: Experiment with writing "environmentally driven" stories where the setting reacts to the audience's presence.

2. Audience-Driven Content Creation
A. AI-Powered Audience Analysis
Platforms like Netflix use AI to predict audience preferences, guiding content development.
- Example: House of Cards was tailored based on data analytics showing high engagement with political dramas.
- Tip for Writers:
  - Use audience data to align your script's themes and tone with popular trends while keeping your unique voice.

B. Crowdsourced Storytelling
Social media platforms and online forums are fostering collaborative storytelling, where creators engage directly with their audience.
- Example: The SCP Foundation features stories contributed by a community, creating a shared fictional universe.

3. The Blurring of Genres

Traditional genre boundaries are fading, giving rise to hybrid genres that appeal to broader audiences.

- Example: Get Out blends horror, comedy, and social commentary, redefining what a "genre" film can be.
- Pro Tip: Combine elements of multiple genres in your scripts to create fresh and compelling narratives.

4. AI's Role in Future Storytelling Trends

A. Real-Time Personalization

AI systems can adapt stories in real-time based on audience reactions, creating unique viewing experiences.

- Example: Interactive live streams where audiences vote on outcomes.
- Tip for Writers: Consider how your story can include adaptive elements to engage audiences dynamically.

B. AI-Generated Worlds

AI is advancing world-building, allowing writers to generate detailed settings and environments quickly.

- Example Tool: World Anvil helps writers organize complex story worlds.
- Pro Tip: Use AI tools to map out expansive worlds for sci-fi, fantasy, or historical dramas.

5. Sustainability in Storytelling

Audiences are increasingly drawn to stories that reflect pressing global issues, such as climate change, social justice, and mental health.

- Example: Don't Look Up uses satire to comment on environmental apathy.
- Tip for Writers: Address relevant issues in your scripts while maintaining an engaging narrative.

6. Exercises for Embracing Emerging Trends

- Create a Branching Narrative:
    - Outline a story with at least two major decision points. Write alternate scenes for each choice and test how they affect the story's tone and outcome.
- Blend Genres:
    - Choose two genres (e.g., romantic comedy and dystopian thriller) and brainstorm a concept that combines elements of both.
- Experiment with World-Building Tools:
    - Use a platform like World Anvil or Artbreeder to visualize settings and characters, then incorporate these elements into a scene.

7. Encouragement for Innovators
The future of storytelling belongs to those who embrace change and explore uncharted territory. Every new trend offers an opportunity to create something original and meaningful. Remember:
- Experimentation leads to innovation. Don't be afraid to take risks.
- Your voice matters. Trends are tools, not constraints—use them to amplify your unique perspective.

Conclusion: Shaping the Future of Storytelling
Emerging trends in storytelling reflect the ever-changing landscape of technology, audience preferences, and creative innovation. By understanding and adapting to these trends, screenwriters can craft stories that resonate deeply with audiences and stand the test of time.

The future is brimming with possibilities, and your creativity is the key to unlocking them.

Chapter 29: Conclusion – The Future of AI and Screenwriting

The world of screenwriting is evolving, and AI is at the forefront of this transformation. From idea generation to revisions, from pitching to production, AI has become an indispensable tool for writers who are ready to embrace its potential. But while technology offers incredible opportunities, the heart of every great screenplay remains the same: the human capacity for storytelling, connection, and creativity.

This chapter reflects on the lessons from this book, explores the role of screenwriters in the future of AI-driven storytelling, and provides encouragement for your journey ahead.

1. Key Takeaways from the Book
A. AI as a Creative Partner
- AI is not a replacement for your creativity—it's an amplifier. By using AI tools to refine dialogue, analyze structure, or brainstorm new ideas, you can push the boundaries of your imagination.

B. Building a Sustainable Career
- Leveraging AI for networking, self-publishing, and audience analysis equips you with tools to navigate the competitive screenwriting industry and grow your career.

C. Staying Adaptable
- The integration of AI in storytelling demands adaptability. Writers who balance innovation with timeless storytelling principles will thrive in this evolving landscape.

2. Looking Ahead: The Role of Screenwriters in an AI-Driven World
A. Unique Human Strengths
While AI can generate content quickly, it cannot replicate the depth of human experience, emotional complexity, or cultural nuance. Screenwriters bring:

- Empathy: Understanding the intricacies of human relationships.
- Authenticity: Drawing from personal and shared experiences.
- Vision: Crafting stories that challenge conventions and inspire change.

B. Redefining Collaboration
AI is reshaping the creative process. Writers will increasingly collaborate with AI tools, directors, and producers to craft stories that push technological and narrative boundaries.

C. Expanding Formats
As storytelling formats diversify—interactive media, immersive VR experiences, and AI-driven narratives—screenwriters have the opportunity to pioneer new genres and formats.

3. Challenges and Opportunities
A. Ethical Storytelling

- Screenwriters must navigate ethical considerations, ensuring AI tools are used responsibly and inclusively.

B. Continuous Learning

- As AI evolves, so should your skills. Stay informed about emerging tools, trends, and storytelling techniques to remain competitive and innovative.

C. Amplifying Creativity

- Use AI to enhance your storytelling while preserving your voice. The balance of technology and creativity will define the next generation of great scripts.

4. Encouragement for the Road Ahead
Screenwriting has always been about persistence, passion, and the belief that stories can change the world. As you embrace the tools and insights from this book, remember:
- Your voice matters. No AI can replicate your unique perspective and imagination.
- Every step counts. Whether you're brainstorming your first script or refining your tenth, every effort is part of your growth as a writer.
- The future is yours. With AI as a partner, you have the opportunity to shape the next era of storytelling.

5. Practical Exercises for Staying Inspired
- Reflect on Your Journey:
  - Write a one-page reflection on how AI has impacted your writing process. What have you learned, and what excites you about the future?
- Set Future Goals:
  - Identify three ways you want to incorporate AI into your writing process over the next year.
- Explore Emerging Formats:
  - Research one new storytelling format (e.g., VR, AR, interactive films) and brainstorm a script idea tailored to it.

6. A Final Word: The Power of Stories
At the heart of every technological innovation is the timeless art of storytelling. Stories connect us, inspire us, and help us make sense of the world. As a screenwriter, you hold the power to shape these stories in ways that resonate with audiences across generations.

The future of screenwriting is filled with possibilities. By combining your creativity with the tools and insights from this book, you can turn your ideas into magic and create stories that leave a lasting impact.

Appendix A: Worksheets and Templates

This section provides practical tools to streamline your writing process, enhance your storytelling, and refine key elements of your screenplay. These worksheets and templates are designed to help you develop compelling characters, construct impactful scenes, and map out your story's structure with clarity and precision.

1. Character Development Sheets
Purpose:
Deepen your understanding of your characters by exploring their motivations, flaws, and arcs. These worksheets guide you in creating multidimensional characters that resonate with audiences.
Worksheet Highlights:
- Basic Details:
    - Name, age, occupation, physical traits, and quirks.
- Internal Goals:
    - What does the character want emotionally or spiritually?
    - What drives their decisions throughout the story?
- External Goals:
    - What tangible outcome are they striving for (e.g., winning a competition, saving a loved one)?
- Flaws and Strengths:
    - What internal weaknesses create conflict?
    - What strengths make them relatable or admirable?
- Backstory:
    - Significant events shaping their worldview and motivations.
Example Prompt:
- "What is one secret your character is keeping, and how does it affect their decisions?"

2. Scene Construction Templates

Purpose:

Ensure every scene has a clear purpose, conflict, and emotional resonance. These templates help you craft scenes that advance the plot and deepen character relationships.

Template Highlights:

- Scene Purpose:
  - How does this scene move the story forward or reveal character development?
- Conflict and Stakes:
  - What is at risk for the characters?
  - How does the conflict escalate tension?
- Emotional Beats:
  - How does the scene affect the audience's understanding of the characters' journeys?
- Visual and Auditory Elements:
  - How can the setting, lighting, or sound enhance the mood and meaning of the scene?

Example Prompt:

- "Write a scene where a character achieves their external goal but fails emotionally."

3. Structure Mapping Sheets

Purpose:

Organize your story into a coherent structure using industry-standard frameworks or explore alternative narrative formats. These mapping sheets guide you in visualizing the progression of your plot.

Three-Act Structure Template:

- Act 1:
  - Setup: Introduce characters, setting, and stakes.
  - Inciting Incident: The event that propels the protagonist into the story.
- Act 2:
  - Rising Action: Escalate conflicts and challenges.
  - Midpoint: A major turning point that shifts the story's direction.
- Act 3:
  - Climax: The ultimate confrontation or resolution.
  - Denouement: Wrap up loose ends and provide closure.

Alternative Formats:

- Nonlinear Narratives: Rearrange key events to reveal information strategically.
- Circular Stories: Begin and end with similar moments, highlighting character transformation.

4. Logline and Pitch Crafting Guides

Purpose:

Create concise, impactful summaries of your story to attract producers, agents, or collaborators. These guides provide templates and tips for writing effective loglines and pitches.

Logline Template:

- "[Protagonist], a [description], must [goal] in order to [stakes], but faces [obstacle/conflict]."
  - Example: "A gifted janitor at MIT must confront his past to unlock his full potential and find love."

Pitch Structure:

- Hook: Start with a compelling one-sentence logline.
- Core Elements: Summarize the protagonist, conflict, and stakes.
- Vision: Highlight why your script is unique and marketable.

Exercise:

- Write three variations of your logline, focusing on different aspects of your story. Test them on peers for feedback.

5. Practical Exercises for Using Templates

Exercise 1: Character Journal

- Write a journal entry from your character's perspective during a pivotal moment in the story.

Exercise 2: Scene Redraft

- Use the Scene Construction Template to rewrite an existing scene, focusing on stakes and emotional beats.

Exercise 3: Structure Alignment

- Compare your story's current structure with the Three-Act Template. Adjust scenes to strengthen pacing and tension.

Conclusion: Tools for Streamlining Your Writing

These worksheets and templates are designed to make your writing process more organized and effective, helping you bring your story to life with clarity and impact. Use them throughout your creative journey to refine your screenplay and ensure it resonates with audiences.

Appendix B: Glossary of Screenwriting and AI Terms

This glossary serves as a quick reference for key terms in screenwriting and AI, offering clear definitions and user-friendly explanations. Whether you're new to the field or looking to refresh your knowledge, these definitions will enhance your understanding of the book's concepts.

1. Screenwriting Terms
Act (First, Second, Third)
- The major divisions of a screenplay, often following the Three-Act Structure:
  - Act 1 (Setup): Introduces characters, setting, and conflict.
  - Act 2 (Confrontation): Develops obstacles and raises stakes.
  - Act 3 (Resolution): Brings the story to its conclusion.

Beat
- A single moment or action in a scene that shifts the story or a character's emotional state.
  - Example: A character deciding to confess a secret.

Climax
- The point of highest tension in the story, where the central conflict reaches its peak.

Denouement
- The final resolution of a story's conflict, tying up loose ends and providing closure.

Inciting Incident
- The event that sets the protagonist's journey in motion, disrupting the status quo.

Logline
- A one-sentence summary of a screenplay that highlights the protagonist, goal, stakes, and conflict.
  - Example: "A reluctant hero must lead a rebellion against an empire to save their galaxy."

Subtext
- The underlying meaning in dialogue or action that is not explicitly stated but implied.

Table Read
- A session where actors or readers perform a script aloud to test dialogue, pacing, and character dynamics.

Theme
- The underlying message or central idea explored throughout the story.
  - Example: Redemption, the cost of ambition, or the resilience of love.

Three-Act Structure
- A traditional framework for organizing a story into three parts: Setup, Confrontation, and Resolution.

2. AI Terms

AI (Artificial Intelligence)
- A branch of computer science focused on creating systems capable of performing tasks that typically require human intelligence, such as problem-solving, learning, and creativity.

Audience Simulation
- AI tools that predict how different demographics or audience groups might react to a story's emotional beats or plot twists.

Branching Narrative
- A story format with multiple possible paths or endings based on audience choices. Common in interactive media and games.

Generative AI
- AI systems capable of creating content, such as text, images, or music, based on prompts or patterns.

Machine Learning
- A subset of AI where systems improve their performance on tasks over time by analyzing data.
  - Example: An AI tool learning to identify successful dialogue patterns by analyzing thousands of screenplays.

Natural Language Processing (NLP)
- The technology that enables AI to understand, interpret, and generate human language.
  - Example: Tools like ChatGPT use NLP to generate dialogue or story ideas.

Neural Networks
- AI models designed to mimic the structure of the human brain, enabling advanced pattern recognition and decision-making.
  - Example: Recognizing patterns in successful movie scripts.

Predictive Analytics
- AI-driven tools that analyze data to predict outcomes, such as how audiences will respond to a specific script or scene.

Storyboarding
- The process of creating visual representations of scenes or sequences. AI tools now assist in generating automated storyboards.

Text-to-Speech (TTS)
- AI technology that converts written text into spoken words, often used for table reads or character testing.

3. Practical Tips for Using the Glossary
- While Writing: Refer to screenwriting terms to ensure you're aligning your script with industry standards.
- When Using AI Tools: Use AI-related terms to better understand and leverage the tools available.
- As a Quick Reference: Keep this glossary handy during revisions or collaborative sessions.

Conclusion: Understanding the Language of Screenwriting and AI
This glossary bridges the gap between traditional screenwriting terminology and modern AI concepts, equipping you with the vocabulary to navigate both worlds confidently. By mastering these terms, you'll enhance your ability to communicate your vision and make the most of the tools available to you.

Appendix C: Recommended Tools and Platforms

This section provides a curated list of tools and platforms to help screenwriters streamline their workflow, enhance creativity, and connect with industry professionals. Each recommendation includes a brief description and practical use case to guide you in selecting the best resources for your needs.

1. AI Tools for Screenwriters
A. Brainstorming and Idea Generation
- ChatGPT (openai.com): Generate story ideas, dialogue, and scene concepts through interactive prompts.
  - Use Case: Ask for plot twists or alternate story endings to overcome writer's block.
- Sudowrite (sudowrite.com): AI-powered writing assistant that enhances creativity and generates prompts for expanding scenes.
  - Use Case: Refine character development or add layers of subtext to dialogue.
- Plot Generator (plot-generator.org.uk): A tool for quickly creating plot ideas and outlines.
  - Use Case: Get inspiration for a specific genre or story theme.

B. Script Formatting and Editing
- Final Draft (finaldraft.com): Industry-standard software for screenplay formatting and collaboration.
  - Use Case: Ensure your script meets professional standards for submission.
- WriterDuet (writerduet.com): A cloud-based screenwriting tool for real-time collaboration.
  - Use Case: Co-write scripts with partners or teams seamlessly.
- ProWritingAid (prowritingaid.com): Grammar and style checker with pacing and readability analysis.
  - Use Case: Refine your dialogue and narrative for clarity and impact.

C. Narrative and Structure Analysis
- Plottr (plottr.com): Visualize and outline your story using timelines and templates.
  - Use Case: Plan story arcs and ensure a balanced structure.
- Dramatica Pro (dramatica.com): Software for analyzing and enhancing narrative structure.
  - Use Case: Diagnose plot inconsistencies and refine character motivations.

D. Visual and Auditory Integration
- Runway ML (runwayml.com): AI-powered platform for creating storyboards and visualizing scenes.
  - Use Case: Generate visuals to accompany your screenplay for pitches or previsualization.
- Suno.AI (suno.ai): Create soundscapes and musical motifs tailored to your script's tone.
  - Use Case: Add auditory depth to scenes for immersive storytelling.
- ElevenLabs (elevenlabs.io): AI-based voice generator for table reads and character testing.
  - Use Case: Hear how dialogue sounds in different voices before casting.

2. Industry Platforms
A. Networking and Career Development
- The Black List (blcklst.com): A platform for connecting screenwriters with producers and agents.
  - Use Case: Upload your script to gain visibility and professional feedback.
- Stage 32 (stage32.com): An online networking platform for writers, filmmakers, and industry professionals.
  - Use Case: Join webinars, pitch sessions, and connect with potential collaborators.
- Coverfly (coverfly.com): A hub for screenwriting contests, fellowships, and development opportunities.
  - Use Case: Submit your script to gain recognition and career advancement.

B. Script Hosting and Sharing
- Script Revolution (scriptrevolution.com): A free platform for showcasing your screenplays to filmmakers and producers.
  - Use Case: Post your work to attract interest from industry professionals.
- InkTip (inktip.com): Helps writers connect with producers looking for scripts.
  - Use Case: Market your screenplay to an extensive network of potential buyers.

3. Community Resources
A. Screenwriting Forums and Groups
- r/Screenwriting (Reddit): A vibrant online community for writers to share advice, feedback, and experiences.
  - Use Case: Get constructive feedback on your work and learn from fellow writers.
- Facebook Groups: Join niche screenwriting groups like Screenwriters Network or Script Notes.
  - Use Case: Participate in discussions, workshops, and networking opportunities.

B. Industry News and Trends
- Variety (variety.com): Stay updated on entertainment industry news and trends.
  - Use Case: Research what studios and streaming platforms are looking for in screenplays.
- Deadline Hollywood (deadline.com): Breaking news and insights on film and TV production.
  - Use Case: Keep track of emerging trends and industry opportunities.

4. Self-Publishing and Marketing Platforms
A. Publishing Your Screenplay
- Amazon Kindle Direct Publishing (KDP) (kdp.amazon.com): Publish your screenplay as an eBook or paperback.
  - Use Case: Reach a global audience with your independently published work.
- Gumroad (gumroad.com): Sell your screenplay directly to fans or filmmakers.
  - Use Case: Monetize your scripts and supplemental materials.

B. Creating Promotional Materials
- Canva (canva.com): Design pitch decks, promotional graphics, and social media posts.
  - Use Case: Build a professional online presence and market your script.
- Adobe Spark (spark.adobe.com): Create dynamic visuals for pitches and online marketing.
  - Use Case: Enhance the presentation of your script for producers or collaborators.

5. Emerging Tools to Watch
A. Real-Time Story Personalization
- Altered AI (altered.ai): AI-driven tools for creating dynamic, branching narratives.
  - Use Case: Experiment with interactive storytelling formats like games or VR.

B. AI in Pre-Production
- Storyboard That (storyboardthat.com): User-friendly tool for creating detailed storyboards.
  - Use Case: Visualize complex sequences during script development.

Conclusion: Choosing the Right Tools
The tools and platforms in this appendix offer a wide range of applications to support your screenwriting journey. Whether you're brainstorming ideas, refining your script, or marketing your work, the right resources can make all the difference.

Explore these options and integrate them into your workflow to elevate your craft and navigate the industry with confidence.

Appendix D: Example Outputs from AI Tools

This section demonstrates how AI tools can enhance various aspects of screenwriting, from dialogue refinement to scene pacing and emotional beats. By examining these examples, you'll see how AI can provide actionable insights and creative inspiration.

1. Dialogue Enhancements
Original Dialogue:
Character A: "I don't think this is going to work."
Character B: "Why not? It seems fine to me."
Character A: "You don't understand what's at stake."

AI-Enhanced Dialogue (using Sudowrite):
Character A: "This plan is a disaster waiting to happen."
Character B: "Disaster? It's a simple solution."
Character A: "Simple doesn't mean safe. One wrong move, and it all collapses."
Analysis:
- Improved Subtext: The AI-added lines hint at tension and stakes without being overly explicit.
- Enhanced Conflict: Dialogue feels more natural and emotionally charged, adding depth to the interaction.

2. Scene Redraft for Emotional Pacing
Original Scene:
The protagonist enters a dark alley. They hear footsteps behind them. They turn around but see nothing. A cat scurries away, and they sigh in relief.

AI-Enhanced Scene (using ChatGPT):
The protagonist hesitated at the entrance of the dark alley, the dim glow of a flickering streetlamp casting long, eerie shadows. The soft shuffle of footsteps echoed behind them. A cold sweat prickled their neck as they spun around, only to face empty silence. Then, a sudden crash—a trash can toppled by a darting cat—shattered the stillness. Their breath came fast, relief mingling with lingering dread as they hurried forward, the shadows feeling heavier with every step.
Analysis:
- Improved Atmosphere: The AI introduces sensory details (light, sound, physical sensations) that heighten tension.
- Engaging Pacing: The rewritten scene sustains suspense longer, making the payoff (the cat) more impactful.

3. Visualizing Story Pacing and Emotional Beats
Tool Used: Dramatica Pro
- Input: A romantic comedy screenplay with uneven pacing.
- Output:
  - Act 1: Steady emotional buildup.
  - Act 2: Too many lighthearted scenes in a row without raising stakes.
  - Act 3: Abrupt resolution without enough emotional payoff.

AI Suggestion:
- Add a midpoint emotional conflict in Act 2 to break the monotony and deepen character development.
- Extend the resolution in Act 3 with a scene where the protagonists confront their feelings before reconciling.

Before and After Comparison:
- Before: Flat emotional progression in Act 2, weak climax.
- After: Balanced pacing, stronger emotional beats, and a more satisfying conclusion.

4. Subtext and Symbolism Suggestions
Original Dialogue:
Character A: "You always take the easy way out."
Character B: "And you always judge me for it."
AI-Enhanced Dialogue (using ProWritingAid):
Character A: "You know, running away won't solve anything."
Character B: "And staying to fight doesn't make you a hero."

Symbolism Suggested by AI:
- Incorporate recurring imagery of open doors to symbolize choices and consequences throughout the script.
- Use contrasting light and shadow to visually reinforce the characters' opposing mindsets.

Analysis:
- Added Depth: Dialogue now conveys tension with richer subtext.
- Visual Impact: Symbolism provides nonverbal ways to enhance the story's themes.

5. Plot Twist Generation
Input Prompt (using ChatGPT):
- "Generate three plot twists for a heist film where the crew plans to rob a high-tech vault."

AI Output:
- The vault contains a decoy treasure, and the real one is in an unguarded location.
- The crew's leader is secretly working with law enforcement to trap the rest of the team.
- A member of the crew betrays the others, but their betrayal was staged as part of the plan.

Analysis:
- Inspiration: The twists provide a variety of directions for the writer to explore.
- Customization: Each twist can be tailored to suit different tones (e.g., comedic, dramatic).

6. AI-Assisted Scene Consolidation
Original Script:
Two consecutive scenes introduce a mentor figure, followed by a training montage.

AI Suggestion (using ChatGPT):
Combine the mentor introduction and training montage into a single scene where the mentor critiques the protagonist's first attempt at a new skill.

Resulting Scene:
The protagonist struggles to climb a wall as the mentor watches with crossed arms. "You're thinking too much," the mentor says. The protagonist stumbles again, muttering, "Easy for you to say." The mentor chuckles and demonstrates the technique. "Now, try it again, but this time, breathe."

Analysis:
- Improved Efficiency: The combined scene maintains pacing while establishing both the mentor's personality and the protagonist's growth.
- Enhanced Engagement: Interaction between characters adds depth and humor.

7. Voice and Table Read Simulations
Tool Used: ElevenLabs
- Input: A dramatic monologue for a protagonist confronting their past.
- Output:
    - AI-generated voice performances in different tones (angry, regretful, resolved).
- Writer Feedback: The regretful tone revealed nuances in the dialogue that were missing in the written text, leading to a revised version.

Conclusion: Seeing AI in Action
These examples demonstrate the versatility and power of AI tools in enhancing screenwriting. From refining dialogue to visualizing pacing and exploring symbolism, AI can offer fresh perspectives and actionable insights to elevate your storytelling. Experiment with these tools to find the approaches that work best for your creative process.

Final Words: Partnering with AI to Shape the Future

Screenwriting is an art form that has always relied on creativity, innovation, and persistence. As technology advances, artificial intelligence has become an invaluable partner in this process— offering tools that can streamline workflows, enhance storytelling, and spark new ideas. But at its heart, storytelling remains a deeply human endeavor.

1. The Balance Between AI and Human Creativity
AI can do a lot—it can suggest plot twists, refine dialogue, and analyze structure—but it cannot replicate the depth of your unique perspective, experiences, and imagination. Your voice as a writer is irreplaceable, and AI's role is to amplify that voice, not overshadow it.

- AI as a Partner, Not a Replacement: Think of AI as your collaborator—a tireless assistant that can handle repetitive tasks and provide fresh perspectives, leaving you free to focus on the creative core of your story.
- The Human Touch: Audiences connect with stories that reflect the human experience, with all its nuances, imperfections, and complexities. Only you can bring that to your writing.

2. Embracing Innovation and Growth
The integration of AI into screenwriting is not just a passing trend —it's a paradigm shift that's here to stay. Writers who embrace these tools will be at the forefront of storytelling innovation.

- Opportunities for Exploration: AI opens doors to new formats, from interactive narratives to immersive VR experiences. By experimenting with these technologies, you can push the boundaries of what's possible in storytelling.
- Continuous Learning: The tools and techniques you've explored in this book are just the beginning. As AI continues to evolve, so will its potential to enhance your craft. Stay curious, stay adaptable, and keep exploring.

3. Encouragement for the Journey Ahead

Screenwriting is not an easy path, but it's one filled with incredible rewards. Every word you write, every revision you make, and every story you share brings you closer to your goals. With AI by your side, the process can be more efficient and inspiring, but the drive to create must always come from within.

- Resilience Matters: Rejections and setbacks are part of the journey. Use them as opportunities to learn and grow, refining your craft and deepening your commitment to storytelling.
- Celebrate Small Wins: Every completed script, every idea brainstormed, every character brought to life is a step forward. Celebrate these milestones—they're the building blocks of your success.

4. A Call to Action

As you close this book, take a moment to reflect on what you've learned and how you can apply it to your next project. AI offers tools and insights, but the true magic happens when you combine these with your creativity and passion. The future of screenwriting is yours to shape—so go out there, write boldly, and create stories that only you can tell.

- Experiment: Try new tools, explore new formats, and challenge yourself to think outside the box.
- Collaborate: Share your work, seek feedback, and connect with others in the industry. AI may be your virtual partner, but collaboration with fellow writers, directors, and producers is equally vital.
- Dream Big: No story is too ambitious if you approach it with dedication and the right tools. Your creativity, paired with AI, can achieve extraordinary things.

Conclusion: The Future Is Bright

The partnership between human creativity and artificial intelligence marks an exciting new chapter in the art of storytelling. By embracing these tools, you have the power to bring your vision to life more efficiently and effectively than ever before. But never forget: the heart of every story you write is you—your voice, your ideas, and your imagination.

The world is waiting for your stories. Let AI help you bring them to life.